Wise Choices

Universal Principles of Managing Life

G. R. Cooper

Yes, 'n' how many seas must a white dove sail
before she sleeps in the sand?

— Bob Dylan

Contents

Introduction

Common knowledge and sense tell us, *the choices we make determine not only the life we live, but what we become.* Unfortunately, people continue to live, by *choice*, in many ways that are not necessarily good for them. In that regard, humanity will never be perfect, but with enough instilled character and the ability to make knowledgeable and *wise choices*, we can act together to improve our lives and the world around us.

As one admittedly imperfect human, among billions of others, I found myself writing this book at the change of a century, as well as a millennium. At the time, optimistically, I felt that we were witnessing the dawn of a truly opportunistic era and the beginning of a, hopefully, more responsible, socially functional world, and realized that our future depended upon the *choices* we, as a society, made from that point forward.

This book is aimed at being a realistic, straightforward, eye-opening look at the rapidly accelerating, constantly changing, and highly challenging world in which we live. I approached writing this from a professional and academic background in the science of management, as well as from lifelong personal experiences and observations. One of my primary motives was the

Columbine school massacre in 1999, which struck close to home for me, since I personally attended one of the high schools located in the same school district as Columbine. Horrified by this incident, and frustrated by other life challenges, I left a full-time career in resort management and entered the public school system as a substitute teacher. I wanted to put my finger on the pulse of the culture surrounding children and education in an effort to get closer to the root problems associated with anger and violence displayed by many youths. I also became a member of the local school district achievement accountability advisory committee in order to obtain an administrative perspective as well.

Of the time I spent substitute teaching, even though I mostly concentrated myself at the high school level, to include alternative schools and correctional institutions, I also covered other levels of education, including elementary and middle school. I did this for the insight and experience of seeing the sociological change process throughout the entire educational spectrum. Over time, I came to the conclusion that there are somewhat predictable biological, psychological, and sociological changes that are occurring in kindergarten through twelfth grade. Something significant happens between the ages of five and eighteen that can be easily witnessed by substitute teaching at all levels, which is a unique frontline observation platform for repetitively viewing these conditional changes.

Much of this book deals with the cause-and-effect relationships that revolve around troubled youth, and where this problem tends to lead the whole of our society, as people grow up and grow older.

Another related motive for writing this book would be all of the corporate scandals in business taking place. Not to stereotype, but take some highly educated boys with misguided values, plant them at the top of major corporations, and watch what happens. It all boils down to a lack of instilled ethics that leads to making unprincipled *choices*.

Within these pages, I have put together a conglomeration of professional and personal perspectives, along with some insightful observations of several controversial issues as they relate to the sociological challenges of life. Should you find some of these issues debatable, I recommend that you keep an open mind while you digest the information presented, and then objectively use your own critical thinking to reach your own personal conclusions. That being said, this book simply becomes additional food for thought in the course of that process.

In order to facilitate positive social changes, you may not find much in the way of political correctness or separation between church and state here. These types of political and religious barriers have been purposely removed in hopes of opening minds and unhampering communications among members of society. Should they become deadlocked in controversy, people simply need to agree to disagree without emotion. Both sides, however, need to intently *listen to* and *respect* the other's points of view. People *have* been known to come to agreements after responsibly opening their minds.

This book is written for all of the open-minded people in the world who are willing to admit human imperfection and make positive changes while committing to knowledgeable and *wise choices* in a new era.

I can only hope that people gain from reading this book a fraction of what I have gained from writing it.

G. R. Cooper

Life Genesis

Born in the U.S.A.

— The Boss

Rumor has it that if you take a frog and put it in a pot of cold water on top of a stove and slowly turn up the heat, the frog will sit there, unsuspecting, until it finally perishes.

Whether anyone realizes or wants to admit it, the world is in hot water. Furthermore, the heat is on. Don't just sit there, Froggy. Do something wise before it's too late!

Unlike frogs, we humans have the ability to visualize a positive future, thereby having the power to *knowledgeably* and *wisely choose* our own fate. It's only when we are skeptical and unethical that we lose control of the means to realistically reach a preferred and desired end.

Historically, though the first human beings may have existed nearly three million years ago with some primitive apelike forms, the Neanderthal cave dwellers, who were somewhat primitive and uncouth, didn't arrive on the scene until around 430,000 years ago. According to limited fossil records, prehistoric modern man came along after that and mysteriously replaced the uncivil Neanderthals about 40,000 years ago.

Archeologists speculate that the Neanderthals may have not been able to compete with modern man, consequently becoming extinct.

Which brings us to more recent history and modern agricultural people who have existed on Earth for the last 12,000 years or so. In this timeframe of human history, the world population has slowly increased, but in just the last two hundred years (less than a blink in geologic time), it has accelerated and grown in astronomical proportions.

According to statistics compiled by the United Nations and the U. S. Census Bureau, by 1987, the world population had reached five billion people. Not long after that, in 1999, as I started writing this book, it surpassed six billion, and by the year 2022, the population had reached eight billion. Like a rocket taking off – from a distance, it barely seems to rise, then accelerates rapidly upward. That's exactly what the earth's population is presently doing – *skyrocketing*.

Currently, the world population is still growing by roughly 175,000 a day, which amounts to around seventy-five million additional people added to this planet each year.

To put it into perspective; it took all of human history, up to the year 1804, to reach a global population of just one billion – metaphorically depicted by the ignition and slow liftoff of our rocket. The second billion folks were on board by 1927. At the current rate, we're adding an additional one billion people approximately every twelve years or so. Think about the magnitude and impact of regularly adding a billion people to a limited world environment.

Given the present trend, provided the earth could let out its belt quick enough, the planet will approach approximately ten billion people by the year 2060 – as our symbolic rocket accelerates out of Earth's atmosphere. Considering the added level of pollution to the world each year, brought about by seventy-five million additional residents, we stand to eventually destroy the environment.

As sure as the sun comes up in the east each and every morning, you can also be sure that a great number of newborn human beings will enter the world before the day is done, above and beyond those who unfortunately perish. You can also be sure that in increasingly highly populated areas, they won't always be getting along with each other. The official term for this I believe is called *Social Tension*. I'm sure that any resulting bad dispositions are not intentional and are simply caused from being around each other a little too much in a crowded and busy environment, day in and day out, ultimately getting on each other's nerves. We do have a *choice* to be civil with each other, but in this ever-crowding world, we frequently *choose* to be increasingly irresponsible and dysfunctional as individuals, families, and organizations. In many cases, rudeness has replaced courtesy, while helpful and kind dispositions have been substituted with bad attitudes. Did you know that the number one complaint expressed by employees in the workforce is rudeness displayed by coworkers? One of the best bumper stickers I ever saw, though somewhat intolerant in itself, simply stated, *Mean People Suck.*

The National Academy of Sciences warns, *"Humanity is approaching a crisis point."*

Like a cool, breezy autumn day in the Rocky Mountain high country, prior to the onset of winter, all of these signs should be alerting us that sweeping change is approaching.

Clearly, the world population, as well as its associated problems, will continue to leapfrog, likely reaching the crisis point that the National Academy of Sciences warns about, unless we wake up and get out of hot water.

In any event, there could certainly be some drastic corrections taking place here on Earth in the future. More than likely, there may be a *series* of these correcting events that could very well act to put the world population back in check.

Being pragmatic, I'd say that not even all of the eternal optimists out there, with their *half-full* glasses, could prevent nature from taking its due course and population correction ultimately occurring. In other words, it's quite clear to see that our rocket may not make it into orbit before it experiences some technical difficulties. Yes, what goes up must indeed come down – it's simply a natural principle that can't, even *optimistically*, be ignored.

On the other hand, this planet, I believe, could possibly survive and support the ten billion people that we'll have on Earth by the year 2050. However, speaking from a background in management science, it will only survive if we can put our prejudices and special interests aside and succeed in advancing ourselves, as a team, to a higher level of wisdom and technology, where limited hydrocarbon-produced energy, chemical wastes, and pollution become a thing of the past. Outside of reaching and implementing this advanced level of society, all we're presently doing is dealing with the increasing population and pollution along with restricted and dwindling resources to the best of our ability with our current technology and lack of wisdom.

Time is of the essence if we expect to turn things around.

Running out of room and resources, added to both natural and man-made catastrophes, we may, indeed, have a combination of some grave problems on our hands. Fortunately, we have *education*, *experience*, and *knowledge* on our side, but the challenges that the world must overcome are difficult at best.

Outside of producing enough food, water

to grow that food becomes a critical concern. Without water, life would cease to exist. Presently, in highly populated areas, the lack of fresh water is the primary thing that will ultimately limit population. There are many large metropolitan areas right now, where water rationing and regulation is an everyday way of life and getting worse. Statistically, global consumption of water is doubling every twenty years, more than twice the rate of human population growth. According to the United Nations, more than one billion people already lack access to fresh drinking water, and the demand for fresh water is rising more all the time. Understand, as this situation unfolds, public water systems in a capitalistic economy will continue to privatize around the world. As they do, there are certain special interests poised to obtain control of these systems, as well as the price of water. What this means is that at some future point, we'll all be budgeting to flush our toilets and take baths, while those special interests rake in billions of dollars selling us potable water.

To further add to the problem, our modern world is using more and more energy to sustain itself. Highly populated regions will be experiencing increasing shortages of electricity every year. Over half of America's need for energy is dependent on fossil fuels, and with other nations developing an appetite for modern data technology, this energy crisis may quickly reach critical proportions. Unfortunately, that currently puts everyone in the world at the mercy of the fossil fuel industry unless we can transition to renewable sources. Climate change may help drive that, but the fossil fuel industry continues to dominate.

Reality dictates that without adequate quantities of fresh water, food, and energy supplies, the world cannot continue to support the predicted population levels.

Add the insanity of rising terrorism and violence to all of this, and we're really pressing the crisis envelope. Suffice it to say, we may need to play that *wisdom* card soon.

Looking back in history, life in the rudimentary North American colonies, prior to the founding of the United States of America, originally set out to provide a desirable and fairly equitable style of life to everyone who worked for it in the context of personal freedom. After becoming a separate nation, the United States, under its original charter, slowly started to reshape and change its system of government.

With the implementation of taxation in 1913, when the average American citizen made about a thousand dollars a year, a form of socialism was adopted as part of the overall scheme of things. Supposedly after one became successful and reached a comfortable level of living, a proportion of the excess fat at the top was to be put back into the economic system. This was done to help keep the entire country strong while reaching out, in common good, to those less fortunate or with limited opportunities. By design, it was to be distributed both fairly and constructively in the form of social services, rehabilitation, education and training, etc.

The only thing that went wrong along the way is that human greed and corruption have since begun to dominate the picture, reshaping that original charter. Today, there are too many overcontrolling lobbyists, large corporations, and special-interest groups manipulating our systems of government – including our tax system. As it stands now, with advanced capitalism, it's technically still a free country, but most of the resources are now rising to the top and staying there, as evidenced by the glut of corporate mergers and acquisitions taking place, not to mention current executive compensation levels and the number of billionaires, multibillionaires, centibillionaires, and the first trillionaires are on the horizon.

Consequently, the poor and middle class are not enjoying quality of life in relation to the upper crust much. More importantly, I'm not sure that where we're headed is good for America. Is this what the forefathers had in mind when they originally laid out the foundations of this country?

Given the vast increase in world population and the decrease in resources, the majority of people continue struggling to make ends meet. The affluent are born with proverbial silver spoons in their mouths, having life also served to them on silver platters. For some, silver isn't good enough; they have to have everything gold. Most people, however, will have to settle for cheap everyday ware, if not their own empty fingers.

From the beginning of history, there has been a perpetual power and wealth struggle between the affluent and the nonaffluent – the haves and have-nots. In a corrupt litigious and political world, guess who's winning?

Fortunately for the lower classes, in the midst of this struggle, there remains a principle called democracy, which by design, coupled with free enterprise, is a fairly good way of life. Throughout the history of democracy, the Free World has condemned certain undesirable forms of government, such as dictatorships, communism, and socialism. These forms of government, without democracy, are a pretty bleak way to live, with produced goods and services strictly regulated by those particular governments to distribute as they see fit.

The catch is, matured capitalism in a democratic society may not be much better when it becomes predatory. With democracy as the greatest form of government the world has ever seen, if there is not a blend of ethics with guaranteed freedom, greed and corruption will inevitably take over the system. Realistically, due to that, no man-made government has ever survived in the long run. So, as it stands, any government will ultimately fail due to the natural and primitive human tendency toward irresponsibility and selfishness.

Benjamin Franklin at the end of the 1787 Constitutional Convention, said to a woman who asked what kind of government the new Constitution had created - He replied; "A Republic, if you can keep it."

The only way any system of government will ultimately succeed is if the vast majority becomes ethically responsible and trustworthy of each other, if that's even possible.

Logistically, only after society realizes and admits its present inability to govern itself in a responsible manner, and commits to change, can change place. Only then will the world reach the required level of wisdom to finally begin to set itself free from its historical social dysfunction. Only then can there be peace.

The affluent upper class in a mature capitalistic society, as you would expect, will emphatically argue that everyone has an equal opportunity to be successful and that *they* worked hard to get where they are. Did they really work any harder than everyone else out there struggling to make a living? I'd say it's more a matter of *brains* overpowering *brawn*. The affluent have mostly been highly educated and, therefore, merely *outsmarted* the rest of the world along the way. The executives, as a prime example, at Enron Corporation, who each skated away with millions of dollars from one of the largest bankruptcies in American history, obviously outsmarted many of their own employees who unfortunately lost their retirement savings as a result. Shortly after that, WorldCom and Global Crossing, among other companies, were found to be cooking the books for billions of dollars as well, leading to economic downfall on Wall Street, as investors lost their confidence and patience in these types of big businesses.

Business, both national and international, has reached a new dimension. The days of immigrants arriving in America with no money, finding opportunity and prosperity, are all but over. According to editorials that I've read, the longer new immigrants stay in America, provided they can stay, the worse off they become, in contrast to the upward mobility of earlier generations, due to the new immigrants' inability to obtain a quality education, mostly impeded by dominant cultures. In fact, the dropout rates in schools among immigrants are three times higher than for native-born Americans. The net effect is social dysfunction. In fact, highly populated cities, having large numbers of immigrants, are now some of the most dysfunctional places in America. The following is just one of many examples taken from the front page of a major metropolitan newspaper:

Drawn by gunfire and their mother's

screams, four pajama-clad children peered through their bedroom window...staring at the aftermath of a shooting that left them orphaned.

The police report indicated that the children's underprivileged father had shot his wife three times, one early October evening. The man then pointed the revolver at his own head and fired one last time. I'll leave you to imagine the circumstances revolving around this incident. Ironically, that fatal shooting came just three days into Domestic Violence Awareness Month. To what kind of life do you think those disadvantaged kids were destined?

Cities might be a good place to live and raise families. Unfortunately, the way things are, they're often not. Why? It takes instilled character and wisdom for large numbers of diverse people to get along with one another. Quality parenting and education become key elements for success and happiness.

Today, with some lucky (in the right place at the right time) exceptions, many established and successful people are at an advantage, being born into political and inherited opportunities.

By whatever means, relative to everyone's basic needs, there are people who earn or possess an excessive amount of money for what they actually do (or don't do), while others are forced to work long physical hours for relatively modest to moderate wages.

In all fairness, there *are* caring and responsible affluent people who generously pay it forward and give back to society in earnest thanks for their own success. My reproach is not so much with them, but with the situation of excessive power and wealth leading to corrupt greed in general.

It's great to become successful, but financially, things have become too far out of balance – especially when it's the poor consumer that has to ultimately foot the bill.

Additionally, there are some real blue-sky situations unfolding around entertainment and professional sports, with multi-million-dollar contracts becoming commonplace, creating a situation that has gotten way out of hand.

People need to stop putting business, entertainment, and sports celebrities on pedestals. They're just human beings like the rest of us. So, they're talented, that's great, but idolizing them just goes to feed their egos as well as their bank accounts.

Where will the cost of business and entertainment and the obsession with sports ever end? It will end when people gain enough self-discipline to stop feeding expensive supply with obsessed demand.

To its credit, considering the important physical fitness and teamwork values found in sports, I think athletics serve a vital function in our public schools and colleges to keep energetic young people off the streets and out of trouble. However, the thrill of victory quickly turns to the agony of celebrity. Men, for example, who played football for the sport of it in school, now play for major league teams that are big businesses. With baseball, women and children used to be *taken out to the ballgame* on Sunday afternoons to watch legends like Micky Mantle and Babe Ruth dedicate themselves to a *sport* rather than a giant paycheck. Today, it's all aimed at huge amounts of money, with games scheduled practically every afternoon or evening, in stadiums that can't be built without the financial influence of large corporations. Additionally, tickets and amenities to attend professional sporting events have become so expensive that a lot of people simply can't enjoy that luxury anymore. Many people are getting fed up with and are now boycotting this situation. Even some of the players can hardly believe the compensations of their contracts.

By comparison, teachers, police officers, and firefighters, who put their lives on the line every day, don't make a fraction, throughout their entire careers, of some of these outlandish contracts. We all have to make a living somehow; however, no one needs to make a *killing* at the expense and exploitation of everyone else.

As an example of corporate exploitation of people, without regard to their welfare, the three most popular substances sold in popular consumer products are nicotine, caffeine, and alcohol. Realistically, *none* of them are good for us, and *all* of them just happen to be highly addictive. Nicotine has been found to be far more addictive than heroin. In fact, cigarettes kill almost a half a million people a year in the United States. Alcohol has destroyed many lives as well.

What should all of this be telling us? With large corporations exploiting and addicting so many people for the sake of their bottom line, is it any wonder why there's so much public apathy? Additionally, these businesses are questioning why they have such a difficult time keeping and motivating good employees. Average people are beginning to seriously question the importance of working so hard.

Society needs to take a long, hard look at its value systems. Perhaps excessively compensated people should find themselves not in the *Land of Oz* anymore, but back in *Kansas* as moderately paid public service and social workers. From the appearance of the way many of them are living their lives, it would probably humble them and bring them back to reality. Even *wizards* have been known to change and come back to earth.

At the beginning of a capitalistic system there may be equal opportunity, however, as the system advances and develops, the rich just keep getting richer, and the poor people end up having to work in relatively low-paying occupations. Many of them find themselves stuck in a rut while working unchallenging, non-meaningful jobs to barely pay their rents or mortgages to the wealthy landlords sitting on the other side of the economic tracks.

With advanced capitalism, there are now more billionaires and millionaires in the world than ever before – most of them living in the United States. Be it Amazon, Meta, Microsoft, Tesla, or Walmart, even the business laws in America have a hard time going up against such rich and powerful organizations. It's pretty scary when money becomes more powerful than government.

In the year 2000, there were somewhere around 250 of billionaires in the United States. By 2020 there were over 700 of them. Today, there are around a thousand. *Forbes Magazine* doesn't even bother listing millionaires anymore. Wealth and power have reached a frightening dimension.

As Mahatma Gandhi once said; *"The world has enough for everyone's needs, but not everyone's greed."*

Even our television programs are becoming obsessed with wealth, power, and immorality. Since the turn of the recent century, the world has been inundated with what is now referred to as *Reality TV*. Mostly younger audiences seem to be obsessed with highly popular shows such as *Survivor* and *Weakest Link*. Many of these forms of entertainment, although a notch above some sitcoms, display little decency or virtue while humiliating guests, for which Diane Sawyer of ABC was once quoted as saying; *"Bottom line – this is the end of Western civilization."* Additionally, Charles Gibson had commented that these shows are the *"commercialization of cruelty."*

What kinds of people enjoy seeing others rejected, intimidated, humiliated, and hurt? In the ailing arena of our own entertainment, the lust for wealth and power, along with a declining morality has taken over love and respect for each other.

Sadly, with all of the billionaires and millionaires that exist today in the richest nation on Earth, there are still tens of millions of Americans living in poverty and many kids going hungry every day. Obviously, upper society cares more about money than it cares about underprivileged children.

Home prices have jumped so high in America that too many families are having trouble finding affordable housing. Increases in family income levels have trailed the rise in home prices, even though the number of dual-income households has increased. Families are being forced to devote more and more of their income to housing. Wages never seem to catch up.

It was Jimmy Carter who pointed out that in 1900, people in the ten-richest nations earned nine times as much per capita as did people in the ten-poorest nations. By 1960, the ratio was thirty to one, and by 2001, it was seventy-two to one. Comparatively, about half the people on Earth now live on less than $2 a day. By another account, the richest people on Earth have wealth that far exceeds the GDP of many of the poorest nations. At that, the wealthy should be putting themselves in the shoes of the poor – provided the poor even *have* shoes.

I've often heard others comment that they're tired of hearing about the poor, unfortunate people in the world, and that poor people, especially in America, have every opportunity to get ahead in the world if they would just apply themselves.

Hogwash! Or perhaps we should say *frogwash*.

What would happen if you took people with that type of attitude and put them in an environment where they had no money or capital assets, no credit rating, no political influences or contacts, little to no education, and no business sense or experience whatsoever. We'll leave out the lack of confidence and self-esteem that typically goes along with being underprivileged. There's a big difference between owning the company store and powerlessly owing your soul to it.

Don't get me wrong – I'm not saying that people shouldn't be prosperous. After all, that has always been the *American Dream* – like baseball, mom, and apple pie. What I *am* saying is that once there, they shouldn't take wealth and prosperity for granted, as long as there are children in the world who don't have enough to eat. Additionally, there are honest, hardworking people (taxpayers) that can't afford but desperately need medical and dental services. In this situation, they have no choice but to go without while letting their health and teeth deteriorate.

On the other hand, we've all heard the saying; *If you got it, flaunt it.* Not referring to wealthy people who actually care and contribute generously to society, but there is a part of affluent, world-traveling America that has become spoiled rotten, leaving an arrogant and snobby impression wherever it goes. It's possibly one reason why the rest of the world hates Americans so much. Have you read *The Ugly American*, written by William J. Lederer and Eugene Burdick? It was a best-seller whose title became a synonym for what was wrong with American foreign policy.

As for the myth of equal opportunity in today's world, anyone with a pea-sized business brain knows that without the magic combination of political contacts, educational knowledge, and ample investment capital, most people rarely achieve anything significant. Realistically, with some lucky or rare exceptions, the vast majority of the poorer people in the world are destined to a life of relative scarcity, no matter *how* hard they work. Perhaps certain affluent and powerful people know that, and due to their scarcity mentalities, poor and powerless is exactly where they want non-affluent people to remain. Either that or they're just indifferent to it.

The gap between rich and poor is growing fast, and the cost of living for the poor and middle class continues to be more than they can afford. Additionally, people (many of them elderly) on fixed incomes are being swindled when it comes to the cost of health services and prescription drugs.

In these situations, the medical, pharmaceutical, and insurance industries add up huge profits, but the poor consumer ends up taking a financial beating while sometimes having to make hard choices between health services and food.

Furthermore, there are people throughout the world who can't afford health insurance, so they often dangerously go without. Here in America, if not for the *Affordable Care Act*, passed by Congress in 2010, tens of millions of Americans would not be covered by any health insurance.

With the haves against the have-nots, financial status has been built into our lives for centuries. The scarcities of available resources have alienated or separated men and women, states and countries, since the beginning of recorded time. The resulting greed and corruption that comes from it has caused the majority of political suffering and pain throughout the world, and the culture has been dominated by perpetual power struggles. Be it men against women, whites against people of color, rich against poor,

Catholics against Protestants, Arabs against Jews, or back to politics, right-wing conservative Republicans against left-wing liberal Democrats, it often boils down to irresponsible behavior.

With the current divorce rate, many families have a power struggle or internal feud going on too. Unfortunately, the damage done to relationships in these situations is always tragic and often irreparable, especially when children are involved.

Scientifically and religiously speaking, there are ongoing debates as to whether life was created or if it slowly evolved. The wise choice here I believe is both, because evolution itself must have been created too. People argue and debate over many things, like the Irish Catholics and Protestants trying to figure out just what it is *they're* actually fighting over. Or how about the never-ending religious turf war fought between the Jewish Israelis and the Islamic Palestinians? And of course, back to politics, let's not leave out the power struggles that go on between the Democrats and the Republicans in Congress. Having the experience of being a teacher, I can honestly say that I've seen first and second graders act more responsibly with each other compared to our elected representatives.

As for the year 2000 U.S. presidential election between Bush and Gore, as I had begun writing this book, I wondered at the time if America's best interest was being considered.

With that particular election, all the way to the Florida State Supreme Court, as well as the U.S. Supreme Court, we, the people, proved our incapability of objective and impartial government. Even U.S. Supreme Court Justice John Paul Stevens, in writing the major dissent, indicated that the decision was a political calamity for the court. In it he wrote:

Time will one day heal the wound to that confidence that will be inflicted by today's decision. One thing, however, is certain. Although we may never know with complete certainty the identity of the winner of this year's presidential election, the identity of the loser is perfectly clear. It is the nation's confidence in the judge as an impartial guardian of the rule of law.

Unfortunately, it was not the *popular vote* of the American people that determined the forty-third president of the United States. Due to the Electoral College, the majority doesn't count.

With all of the bickering and fighting going on in the world, there are certain things that we should be wise enough not to argue about. At that, we should stand back and look objectively with critical thinking and understanding. Creation and evolution would be a classic example of one of those debatable arguments.

It's obvious, at least to me, that both creation and evolution have actually had to exist in unison. The scientific world has already proved, even though others keep refusing to accept it, that evolution is a fact. There is simply far too much geologic and biologic evidence to support it. With that in mind, the universe and matter itself had to have come from somewhere. It didn't just…POOF…all of a sudden come to exist out of nothing all by itself. It's quite clear that the whole scheme of things has been miraculously well planned and managed from the very genesis of time as we know it. We need only to look around, to see the extremely complex level of planning, organizing, directing, and controlling – in a word, *management* – that is required to keep all umpteen-jillion balls precisely juggled every nanosecond of every day. You don't need to be a scientist to see this perfectly managed system of physics and nature being orchestrated to a maestro's perfection. Like evolution, it's just too obvious; that is, as long as one wisely chooses to see these universal truths.

At that, we should stop debating as to which came first, the chicken or the egg. It stands to reason both were not only created but were created as products of evolution and will continue to evolve as sure as the world itself. In that respect, evolution had to have been created as well. It, *too,* didn't just begin to happen all by itself.

With that reasoning out of the way, I still have to wonder just whom or what this divine being or intervening, universal governing force might be. After contemplating that question most of my life, I suppose the precise answer will be experienced at the end of life. Who truly knows what or who it is, but I strongly believe, beyond a shadow of my own doubt, that there is a superior being or force out there, call it God if you will, driving all of this in a well-managed, highly complicated, and super-technological manner. To think it all just *happened* in the face of scientific evidence is frankly naïve.

Closer to home, one of the greatest miracles, so commonplace we barely think about it, would be the actual *conception* as part of the creation and evolution of human life, or as this chapter suggests...*life genesis*. The conception and birth processes are proportionately just as complicated and intricate as the workings of the universe itself. The timing of the complex chemistry, biology, physics, and genetics required to produce a human being is far beyond chance and circumstance.

After conception and nine months of incubation, the newborn arrives to greet the world. Following a period of rolling and crawling around haphazardly, the child will eventually rise to stand on its own wobbly legs. This young human being has now achieved a vertical stance, only to find itself politically postured and waiting in line with billions of others for anything it wants or needs from that moment on. Additionally, this fledgling will soon begin to develop a primitive but useful vocabulary by uttering its first words…mommy…daddy…and…Mine! He or she has now suddenly and naturally adapted to a competitive world of perceived scarce resources.

Related to scarce resources, political posturing and overpopulation, from a systems management perspective, every undesirable situation is the direct result of a series of symptomatic problems brought about by certain root problems. The primary symptomatic problem, in the case of overpopulation, would be unneeded or undesired offspring. This is brought about by a secondary symptomatic problem of unmanaged conception. It is therefore clear that the root problem is, in fact, a lack of instilled wisdom at the actual time of conception. That is, abstinence and/or being of age and practicing responsible birth control.

I can understand religious positions to be plentiful and to multiply in abundance. However, with billions of people in this world fighting over limited resources, each yelling, *MINE*, there comes a time to be sexually wise and responsible.

Considering legalized abortion as the result of the famous Supreme Court case of *Roe v. Wade* that took place in the early 1970s, it took our highest legislative process to have to rule in such a personal and private matter, and to later undue it. Fact of the matter, there are way too many unwanted babies being born into the world, and for unwanted babies, prevention is always the best medicine, that is, education, abstinence, or birth control. Other than that, I have no misgivings concerning early, first trimester abortions if necessary, using FDA approved medications or AMA approved medical procedures. Unfortunately, with such a sensitive issue, it seems as though people can never agree on anything anymore without letting religious ideologies and political biases get in the way.

To paraphrase an analogy that was used by highly respected management expert Steven Covey, there is no moral compass being observed in society that points each and every human in the same ethical direction, regardless of biases. Covey indicated:

Ultimately the successful implementation of any strategy hinges on the integrity people have to the governing principles and on their ability to apply those principles in any situation, using their own moral compass.

Sad to say, unethical ideologies and special interests have become the all-too-commonplace standard and status quo. It can be argued that abortion is unethical, to which I would say bringing unwanted babies into the world is just as bad if not worse. Again, prevention is the best medicine for that.

Ideally, we need to wise up and turn things around. I can imagine others saying, *don't be so idealistic.* To that I would argue that it has little to do with idealism and much to do with solid values and principles in conjunction with ethical management practices. As for idealism, the concept does in fact exist, and it could very well be brought to fruition if we'd only allow it. Unfortunately, it has not been permitted. Idealism is a highly suppressed concept, rejected by unprincipled people dealing with situations with which they would personally rather not take ethical responsibility. If people weren't so non-ideal at times, ridiculed idealism would have a fighting chance at becoming reality, causing the world to become more of an *idealistic* place to live.

For most people, their lives probably have yet to be associated with the word *ideal*, but hopefully they were fortunate enough to be raised with enough *ethics* to have given them the integrity and character they need to conduct themselves *honorably* in society.

As we conclude this chapter, it should be said the United States of America has remained one of the greatest nations on Earth. However, its status stands in jeopardy with the rest of the Free World. It now becomes a *choice* whether to accept and continue the failing status quo or to transcend into unified nations of a New World, bound closer to a realized idealism commonly envisioned as *Paradise* and *Peace on Earth*. Otherwise, like the way of the dinosaurs, or frogs, it may be the final curtain for humanity. It all boils down to a matter of *choice*.

Innocent Children

Forever Young

— **Rod Stewart**

There's a distinct innocence, gleaming happiness, genuine trust and love associated with young children. Sadly, many soon become the victims of human society.

One in ten children in America suffer from *serious* mental and emotional disturbances. By no fault of their own, many of these kids consequently land in the lap of our juvenile justice and correction systems. Unfortunately, they're usually a day late and an innocent life short when they do.

Members of society may point the finger of blame at previous generations or at public education or even the juvenile justice systems for noneffective education and correction. In return, those segments may reactively point *their* fingers at the government, social services, and insurance companies for not covering emotional disturbance and mental illness, as they should.

The science of management tells us that the root of the problem is none of the above. If many of the mentally and emotionally disturbed kids today had been exposed to principled lives, we wouldn't have the *need* to put them through juvenile justice systems or to treat them for emotional disturbances and mental illnesses so much. At that point, society could put all the money it's wasting on futile correction efforts back into basic health and education where it belongs, instead of chasing symptomatic tails.

Additionally, perhaps it's time for people to stop blaming the schools for a lack of security and start taking full responsibility for why emotionally disturbed kids are bringing guns to school in the first place. Again, we wisely need to focus on the root problems and quit stabbing at the symptoms. Outside of genetics, which *can* be a factor, the basic problems here involve such things as drug and alcohol abuse, domestic violence, divorce, broken homes, and the fundamental lack of instilled character in certain parents as well as their kids. The heart of the problem can often be found in the quality of parenting. The fire will never go out until we learn to control the source of fuel that's feeding it.

Children are exposed to and learn everyday human politics adults and peers teach them, often through example, such as playing favorites or making fun of others, bullying, backbiting and gossip, just to name a few. These actions can be further categorized under symptoms such as jealousy, greed, prejudice, and hate caused by a deficiency of instilled ethics, which again mostly point to the root problem as being the lack of principle-centered values, often instilled by parents.

Here's a concern coming from a fourteen-year-old student, Niko, expressed to his parents: *"Don't keep saying do as I say, not as I do. Like it or not, I learn from what you do!"*

Relative to setting good examples while teaching and instilling principles in young people, I was substituting eighth-grade history one day when my only pencil disappeared from my desk in the back corner. This apparently happened while I had my back turned and was writing on the board at the front of the room. Later, while looking for my pencil, I addressed the class and asked whoever took it from the desk to please return it. There was no response. A second time, I asked whoever took the pencil to kindly return it. Still little response, except for some of the students commenting on the fact that it was only a stupid pencil that I was getting upset about. Well, at that point, I paused for a moment before I spoke. Whether they wanted to hear it or not, and they didn't, I proceeded to explain that stealing a pencil is just as bad as stealing a million dollars. This resulted in an unprecedented level of criticism erupting from one particular male student. While ignoring this outburst, I continued by saying that granted, the monetary *values* of the crimes are vastly different but that in *principle* there is no difference whatsoever, and that principles come without a price tag. I then went on with the class, again turning my back and continued to write on the board. When I finished, one of the female students suddenly pointed out to me a yellow pencil on the floor under a table on the opposite end of the room from where it had disappeared. She theorized that the pencil must have rolled off of the desk and clear across the room where it was now resting. I commented that that must have been the case and apologized to the entire class for my ignorant misperception and for thinking that any of them could have possibly taken the pencil in the first place. The class subject matter that day was history; however, the real lesson was on values and principles.

The science of management tells us that what is sorely missing throughout the world is quality education and the instilling of proper character and integrity in young people. Moreover, it is the responsibility of all grownups to guide and mentor children by setting good examples.

Further considering values as well as principles, people normally either center their lives on values, or they center their lives in principles. Everyone *has* or needs both, at least to a certain degree, but the key is which of the two are at the *center* of *your* life – values or principles? Steven Covey, mentioned earlier, also talks about this in his books – the best-known being, *The 7 Habits of Highly Effective People*.

Values can be things like family, friends, and creative occupations. They can also be money, expensive cars and houses, fame, status, clothes, jewelry, etc. On the other hand, principles are things like dignity, ethics, self-discipline, patience, and honesty. Principles are also traits that can be characterized by integrity, kindness, responsibility, trust, etc. See the difference between values and principles? So, which do you think we should be teaching and modeling to children? We all know the answer, don't we? So why do we resist what we know is true?

It was Sir Winston Churchill who said, *"Most people, sometime in their lives, stumble across truth. And most jump up, brush themselves off, and hurry on about their business as if nothing had happened."*

Our lives not only need but also *must* be centered in principles to be full and complete and to obtain meaning. They simply can't be centered on values alone. Even though values are required in our lives, we should not center ourselves totally on them (especially false values). If we do, we will more than likely go through life with this gnawing feeling in our stomachs – like there's something wrong but we can't quite put our finger on it. That feeling is a lack of principle-centered living.

You may be surprised to learn that centering your life strictly on family, above and beyond principles, doesn't work either. Again, family is a *value*. It can certainly be a *primary* value, but it can never take the place of a principle-centered life. I have known people who center their lives on family but who are still lacking strong character traits.

Focusing on values, instead of principles, won't get you where you need to be, no matter how much money and power you acquire along the way, and you can't compensate by coercing or manipulating your way through life either.

Considering our current society, people don't have to subject each other to negative and exploitive politics. It's certainly not required as a condition of civilization by any means. Many simply *choose* to do it. We've already discussed part of the reasoning being jealousy. We'll be discussing other contributing factors as we continue through the book. At this point in human history, however, instinct for survival can no longer be used as an excuse – that reasoning should have ended with the Neanderthals. Nevertheless, the politics and false values continue in modern society.

In this type of environment, something slowly happens to many innocent children as they become exposed to other humans and the omnipresent dysfunction of human society – the defensive shields start to rise. And when those shields are not strong enough to hold out troubled waters, mental and emotional illness floods in to drown them. Outside of ignoring the problem and doing nothing about it, which happens every day, parents, who can afford it, often pass their kids off to the professional social systems available to them. Unfortunately, the lower classes don't get what they can't begin to pay for. As a result, due to the system, 10 percent of our kids become tragically lost, as was mentioned at the start of the chapter.

Many children are the victims of child abuse and neglect. A report released by the National Center for Injury Prevention and Control estimates the annual costs associated with confirmed cases of child maltreatment (physical abuse, sexual abuse, psychological abuse, and neglect) are nearly $500 billion. Isn't it a shame that we can't be productively applying a major portion of those funds toward additional education for both the kids and their parents? If we could turn things around, we might finally be able to attack the root sociological problems of our society.

Another valid option would be for adults to quit teaching divisive behavior to children. This option is actually realistic and possible, but with the world the way it is, we quickly expose children to an environment of dissension where they often begin to display forms of dysfunctional behavior themselves.

This vicious circle exists and survives throughout the world, from one generation to the next, basically unchecked and consequently never extinguished. It's an intensifying fire now almost out of control, which will never burn itself out as long as there is a perpetual source of fuel feeding it. Like any fire, take away the fuel (in this case, dysfunction and the lack of genuine love and respect), and it would fizzle out.

It's too bad we can't just remove children from all the politics and abuse, right after birth, before others start to corrupt them with misinformation, unethical behavior, and nonfunctional human relations. It's a shame we can't keep them away from our current society while educating them outside of any political and prejudicial arenas until they're fully grown with optimum ethics, integrity, and character. If we could do that for just one generation, we might once and for all break the perpetual chain of prejudice and hate that plagues the world and finally begin to open the doors of human relations to pervasive and lasting world peace.

Another more realistic alternative is widespread sociological education (i.e., social studies, psychology, ethics, etc.). That is, educating all of society to a point of full understanding and knowledge of just how unenlightened we are in dealing not only with our children and each other, but also with ourselves, due to a lack of self-awareness. In psychology, self-awareness can be considered the stepping stones to mental stability. From the vantage point of knowledge and mental stability, society can then further educate itself to the next level while implementing the real solutions to our sociological problems. Therefore, education and knowledge are the keys to unlocking this door.

With this type of widespread education teaching self-awareness and self-correction, social dysfunction could be finally checked. Only through education can we change because we *want* to and not because we *have* to.

Making others aware of these problems, while learning myself, is actually one more reason I had for writing this book. I've already admitted *I'm* not anywhere *near* perfect. That doesn't mean that I'm not aware of the social challenges we face. I'm fully aware that we're not going to solve all of our problems overnight, but we seriously have to get it in gear at some point. I'm confident that one day, provided we don't destroy ourselves in the meantime, the world can get to where it needs to be and eventually turn the tide of prejudice and hate into love and respect. That would be a *wise choice.*

Materialism and greed are classic examples of non-principle-centered behaviors that children are exposed to. It all starts out with toys. Thoreau described it by saying, "*Our inventions are wont to be pretty toys, which distract our attention from serious things.*"

I can still remember one of my very first toys. It was a small plastic figure of *Mr. Peanut.* My parents, being poor at the time, probably couldn't afford much else.

A child, before it starts to reason, doesn't need expensive objects to keep him or her amused and happy. It's not until we are exposed to media, mixed with politics, that we then seem to need more costly things.

Children, with the materialistic priorities in their early lives being somewhat limited, battery-operated toys are not required to be happy. Personally, I think kids become much more creative and resourceful having simple toys or the boxes they come in. Furthermore, it seems that many parents today deprive their children of *longing* for things, which has a lot to do with built-in appreciation. Kids can't and will never fully appreciate anything that they never longed for and had to work for, no matter what the cost, or how *cool* it might be.

We often hear parents say; *My kids are going to have everything that I never had.* Would that include character, ethics, and integrity?

Here's a primary principle of managing life: *The absolute, very best that parents can possibly give to their children are good values and principles – let them work for the rest.*

Seems many kids today have expensive things handed to them at Christmas or birthdays, with the givers hardly getting a *thanks*. As time goes on, kids in this situation rarely get excited over anything, but become masters at showing non-appreciation for not getting exactly what they wanted or what they may have expected. Frankly, they become spoiled, having everything just handed to them.

I once had a conversation with a senior vice president of one of the companies I worked with, and I asked him why it was that he spent so much time at the office. His answer was something to the effect that he had kids that needed to go to college. With that, I wanted to mention that I put myself through college, without parental assistance, but decided it best to mind my own business. At the time, I wondered if his kids were actually getting enough of what they may have really wanted and needed from him – that is, *quality time* and *valuable mentoring*.

Innocent children don't remain innocent forever. By the time they reach their terrible twos, they may not know the meaning of life but are starting to figure out what punishments are all about. Those first disciplinary events, as a form of behavior modification, to get them to do what the big and powerful people want, have something to do with some of the sociopolitical subject matter of this book. This is where kids are in the early stages of being taught functional ethics and the differences between good and bad. At this stage, children may not completely know the difference between what is socially acceptable and what isn't, but undoubtedly, they will have the rest of their lives to figure it all out and to further learn those types of politics.

I'm sure that despite all the free time innocent children have on their hands, most never fully contemplate the origins of the universe, or debate if we human beings are the products of creation or evolution. These are later lessons and concepts introduced by the great and wise educators of the world, otherwise called grownups – many of them professional teachers.

Very young children hardly realize where food, clothing, and shelter come from, let alone what philosophy and science is all about. Food, clothing, and shelter, the basic necessities of life, or more formally referred to as *physiological* needs, are just things most small kids, outside of the third world and our own underprivileged, take for granted.

In the early stages, children lead somewhat sheltered existences with certain barriers and boundaries. Additionally, they are mostly ignorant of the world around them and have a lot to learn in the process of growing up. Being somewhat confined within their new worlds, children approach the stage of excitedly pointing at things they have never experienced, while loudly exclaiming; *What's that?* or *Why?* at least a hundred times a day.

It's not long before a child's sheltered and protected environment starts to expand. What a marvelous and fascinating world there is for them to explore. They just have to be taught to be careful while doing it. Don't touch! Easier said than adhered to.

Not understanding or practicing prejudice as yet, younger children become fascinated that there are other people of all shapes, sizes, and colors in the world. If you watch them, kids are extremely happy to interact with these diverse individuals, supporting the reasoning that people are not born with but are taught to be prejudiced.

The following lines are from the classic Rogers and Hammerstein's play *South Pacific*:

> *You've got to be taught to hate and fear,*
> *You've got to be taught from year to year,*
> *It's got to be drummed in your dear little ear,*
> *You've got to be carefully taught.*
>
> *You've got to be taught before it's too late,*
> *Before you are six or seven or eight,*
> *To hate all the people your relatives hate,*
> *You've got to be carefully taught...*

Regardless of the habits kids are taught, we adults are responsible for teaching them and need to take that responsibility seriously.

While learning, good or bad, the list of places and objects for little kids to explore are virtually unlimited. It's sad how life seems to lose a lot of that exciting level of exploration when we grow older. Remember that feeling? Where did it go? What happened?

Then there are the important holidays to consider from a child's viewpoint – Christmas, Easter, Fourth of July, and, of course, Halloween. Remember how much fun it was waiting for Santa, going on egg hunts, waving sparklers, or walking down the streets of the neighborhood dressed as skeletons, ghosts, witches, and goblins, partaking in a candy ritual? Except for an upset stomach and having to go to the dentist, at that age, life was good. However, along with stomachaches and dentist drills, it doesn't take long for kids to realize a very valuable lesson and another wise principle of managing life – like too much candy; *if it seems too good to be true, it probably is*. This is a universal principle we all experience but seem to have a hard time learning in order to not continually repeat the same mistakes.

It's funny how, later in life, we go back to some of the very same places we experienced while growing up and marvel at just how small everything actually is from our previous childhood perspective.

It was halfway through my life, while attending graduate school and studying management, that I had what is called a *paradigm shift* and learned an extremely valuable lesson of managing life; *True reality does not exist in any mortal mind, only perceptions*. No matter how much we're convinced we're right, we may actually be wrong. Here's a little exercise that demonstrates this principle:

Take this common yet simple math test; do it in your head and don't use a calculator.

Take 1,000 and add 40 to it. Now add another 1,000. Now

add 30…

Add another 1,000. Now add 20. Add another 1,000. Now add 10.

So, what's the total?

Now go back and double-check it, just to be sure.

Did you get 5,000 both times?

You're confident you know the answer now, aren't you?

Sorry, the correct answer is actually 4,100.

Don't believe it? Check it with your calculator!

Our minds were preprogrammed, three times, to believe we were going to the next thousand, so we just assumed that 4,090 plus 10 was 5,000.

Our previous experiences in life lead us to believe a perceived reality, when that perception is usually flawed. The world all of us *think* we see is actually a skewed misperception of reality.

Some perceptions are closer to reality than others, but like the concept of perfection itself, nothing, except perhaps the forces behind nature are ever quite perfect. That means that the thought processes of the human mind are also imperfect. We just proved that in the above exercise.

So why do you think kids grow up thinking what they think? The reason being they are highly influenced or *brainwashed* by others.

Experiencing relationships, children begin to realize that relationships between people are not always consistent. They will have different relationships with their mothers than they have with their fathers, or with their siblings. The relationships with people that they know outside of the family are even more different, and relationships to people they don't know – well, children are told they're not supposed to talk to strangers. In that respect, little kids are indirectly taught that they're not to trust people they don't know. If you stop and think about it, this really doesn't do much to get society off to a good social start with one other. If we could all grow up with the genuine ability to trust others, then perhaps people would look at strangers more as *friends* instead of possible enemies. Unfortunately, all it takes is one untrustworthy person to ruin it for everyone else – the bad-apple effect.

Innocent children are often coaxed into situations by their parents that may not actually be in the children's best interest. My mother used to run a small recording studio where she recorded the unique voices of children who were undoubtedly expected by their parents to be the next entertainment celebrities of the world. As I remember, most of them couldn't even carry a tune all that well. To many of the parents of these kids, lack of talent was only a minor obstacle on the way to their child's presumed fame and fortune. I can also remember other parents who would fanatically meddle into their kids' lives, especially in sports, to the point where sports were no longer fun for anyone around them, including the rest of the players, coaches, and other parents. In these situations, parents become bad influences on their kids and a pain in the neck for everyone else. If these parents would just spend as much time coaching their kids in values and principles as they do entertainment and sports, then maybe their kids would have a much better chance of growing up to be someone they could *really* be proud of.

We should keep in mind that success or failure can become a pitfall in life. Fame and fortune? They're probably two of the biggest stumbling blocks when they're aimed at ego and greed. Unfortunately, these traits are often force-fed to children through improper and irresponsible influences.

Yes, innocent children are mostly *taught* bad habits by others, often by example. Greed, prejudice, and hate are probably some of the worst. They are the seeds. Violence and war become the products of those seeds. So, where do children learn to fight and wage war? We've all seen pictures of young boys in other countries sporting militaristic weapons. One can easily understand how the devastation of violence and war carry forward from one generation to the next.

Fear is one of the biggest head-trips there is in life – especially for a kid. Franklin Delano Roosevelt was right when he said, *"We have nothing to fear but fear itself."* Fear is an instinctive, natural trait that helps to keep us out of harm's way. Unfortunately, sometimes it only acts to keep us from actually experiencing life itself. We may survive life, but due to fear, we can also miss out on a lot of it. For example, people's fear of rejection many times keeps them isolated from experiencing the joy of love, just as aquaphobia keeps people from experiencing the joy of swimming, or the way acrophobia keeps people from skydiving. Skydiving is perhaps an extreme example, but still demonstrates the principle I'm referring to. Yes, fear can save lives, but it can also act to suppress certain joyful and rewarding experiences. We can spend our lives as quarterbacks, or we can spend them as *armchair quarterbacks* – it's our *choice*, provided we don't allow fear to dictate.

That wicked, old witch of the West – what a scary hag she was, huh? Other shows back in the old days didn't show graphic violence but were sometimes still scarry to watch. As a child, I remember censored violence still having a frightening impact on me. What kind of impact do you think all of the horror, blood, and guts being produced by today's media is having on kids? Kids are naturally scared of horror and violence, but recent studies done by experts in child psychology support reasoning that children are becoming insensitive to violence. In the same manner, I used to be terrified of heights until I spent a certain amount of time working on aerial tramways. With time and exposure, I slowly became less sensitive to my fear of falling. Additionally, emergency medical professionals are much less likely to freak out over the sight of blood, due to their repetitive exposure in dealing with traumatic incidents. With repetitive exposure to today's less-and-less-censored media, it's understandable how kids are getting insensitive to violence. Now *that's* scary! But then, with all the violent deaths occurring in America's public schools these days, I don't know about you, but I think I'm despondently starting to get used to it...RIBBIT.

When I grew up, it was rare for both parents to work and for kids to be put in day care centers. It was usually the father who went off to work in the morning, while the mother stayed home and cared for the family. Today, it's quite common for both parents to pursue careers or to have to work outside of the home to make ends meet, so child care, along with latchkey kids, has become a standard way of life.

Could we be looking at yet another root cause to our social problems here? Recent studies have indicated that the longer children are exposed to child care, the more aggressive they become. Who knows exactly why, except that the world away from home and away from immediate family can be a very strange and frightening place for young children who have been exposed to today's media. For that matter, it's a strange and frightening place for adults too. And, with over half of all children being subjected to broken homes, stress and emotional disturbance is added. As a society, we can't really blame the children for becoming ticked off at the world. These children simply can't handle the turmoil and emotional pain involved with destroyed family life, added to being dumped off at a day care center each day. Perhaps kids naturally develop aggressive traits when they're backed into these uncomfortable and frightening corners. Animals will do the same thing. Has a strange dog ever growled at you? Or has a strange person in rush-hour traffic ever flipped you off? It's just a natural survival instinct that all animals have, including the human animal.

Considering the above, as children have grown up, past and present, normal or not, is there any wonder why they have always done wild things, like growing long hair or dying it strange colors, piercing and tattooing weird parts of their bodies, wearing odd clothes, or carrying weapons? If not for the need of attention, autonomy, identity, self-protection, and perceived control, they may often do these things out of rejection or intimidation by others.

So, what can parents and adults do to take some of the stress and pressure off? We should each begin by setting a good example while teaching and encouraging young people to make *wise choices*. Grownups need to be careful what they do and say around children. Kids look up to adults as role models, often perceived as heroes, and are highly influenced in behavior as a result. They more often judge adults by who they *are* and what they *do*, rather than what they *say*.

For example, as a child, I idolized my father and spent a lot of time hanging out with him, consequently picking up some bad vocabulary, illustrating the influence grownups have. As I got older, after being threatened to have my mouth washed out with soap, once or twice, I soon cleaned up my vocabulary. Many kids, while not being corrected, will carry foul language into their adulthood where profanity has now become commonplace in general conversations. Just like blood and guts, we all seem to be getting used to it. Does that really make it okay?

School is quite the social experience for innocent children coming from sheltered domestic environments. Those initial years of school are, in effect, a kid's sociological and political training ground. One of these training experiences I recall from my initiation into kindergarten was being shoved around and bullied by some of the older and bigger first-grade boys. The first-grade boys thought they were *too cool for school*, not being in kindergarten anymore, and they used every opportunity to express that superior sociological standing with us inferior pre-graders.

Being one of the smallest kids in my kindergarten class, I was immediately pinpointed as a target by these thugs. My older sister, though, saw what was going on and stepped in to intervene once or twice, giving those first-grade boys a piece of her mind. After all, she was now a second grader, able to put first graders in their place. However, that only proceeded to make things worse for me, because when she wasn't around, I sure got the cold shoulder and several hot elbows by those same bad boys after that.

The very next year, as a first grader, *I* was the upper classman, and it was *my* turn to chew up some of those little kindergarten punks! I actually tried it once and succeeded at scaring one boy half to death. I still feel bad about confronting that innocent little kid back then, for no good reason, other than to pump up my own immature ego – a situation often also modeled to children by grownups.

In any event, that's been my experience dealing with group dynamics, social sparring, and the resulting political and punitive states that kids, big or small, endure in the course of their lives.

All in all, looking back at my own childhood, I can remember a kid that started out happy and full of zest for life but, due to the influence of others, became riddled with fear and uncertainty, often affecting levels of confidence and self-esteem. I believe that I probably developed certain early emotional disturbances due to my childhood surroundings. Sure, we all survive these situations, for the most part, but where does all the grief lead us in life?

I'm just one person who grew up experiencing rejection, abandonment, intimidation, and being bullied. How many more are there? And how many more will there yet be, as the beat goes on? Kids need full parental guidance and reassurance as they face daily problems in the world. Without it, they can't help but to grow up feeling that nobody cares. Clearly, day care centers and broken homes are ill-equipped to provide the unconditional, genuine love and attention that children require.

We, as a society, unknowingly and irresponsibly continue to subject innocent children to this sociological turmoil. As a result, we are now getting exactly the type of mayhem that we're currently seeing unfold at the end of every day on the evening news…RIBBIT.

Formative Youth

The End of the Innocence
— Don Henley/Bruce Hornsby

Research indicates that most of a child's core intellect, personality, and social skills are developed by the age of five. Clearly, these qualities are greatly influenced and determined by life experiences as dealt in those initial years of childhood.

For many, life after that can come with some additional baggage. For me, thank God, I maintained a sense of humor. Many kids, faced with adversity and the pressures of life, tend to lose this quality, as well as their sense of joy. It's then that life can become a dysfunctional tragedy.

After writing his best-seller; *The 7 Habits of Highly Effective People*, Steven Covey wrote another book called *Principle-Centered Leadership* that used the popular phrase; *Give a man a fish and you feed him for a day; teach him how to fish and you feed him for a lifetime.* The main emphasis of *that* particular book was that people should stop living their lives centered on improper values and start living them around tried and true universal principles that have proven themselves among many generations over the course of time. It was a highly-rated book by the readers that actually took the time to read it. Ironically, the last time I looked, the book was out of print, meaning that most people aren't interested in reading a book based on wise principles. To me, that say something.

Basically, it all boils down to adults actually teaching and modeling integrity to kids, as well as other people they may be responsible to, including employees and fellow organizational members. Today, many governments, organizations, schools, and families are in trouble. Double standards have since replaced principles in our homes as well as our private and public organizations. In too many cases, the standards and priorities being expressed to our children or to employees and organizational members are not those being actually lived. Additionally, in many of our corporations, organizations, and schools, those mission, vision, and value statements being published are worlds apart from those being displayed by leadership. It is a fundamental lack of instilled ethics that is at the heart of these double standards and skewed priorities.

According to another well-known and highly regarded management guru, Peter Drucker, the two top traits leaders can possess are *integrity* and *character*. People are not born with these qualities. Integrity and character are features that can only be learned, starting at an early age through principled upbringings. Parenting and leadership are, therefore, a serious responsibility not to be taken lightly.

Concerning recent events in the world such as corporate greed, terrorist attacks, and school or workplace violence, many of us may recognize and acknowledge the problems at hand, yet society seems to be at a loss when it comes to actually solving those problems. Many of us appear to be concerned these days about the direction people, young and old, are going – why they lie, cheat, and steal, and why the populace doesn't seem to know right from wrong anymore. Yes, it may have something to do with childrearing and leadership – the standards and examples set by adults.

By now, it should be obvious to us that the people performing white-collar crimes, terrorist activities, and suicide missions of mass destruction have been reasonably educated and may have learned certain technical skills. Unfortunately, they were never taught ethical values and principles, so their actions are unethical, violent, and *destructive*, rather than ethical, peaceful, and *constructive*. Without instilling decent standards and integrity, intelligence can actually backfire and work *against* society. That intelligence, without a foundation of ethics, does not serve the rest of humanity well.

We should be asking ourselves: if basic values and principles are not currently being taught in the home, then where does the next educational opportunity present itself to society? It presents itself primarily in public education and extracurricular activities. As for true accountability in education, *ethics* should be a prerequisite to, as well as a priority over, math and science. Unfortunately, that's usually not the case.

Improper values, centered in materialism, seem to have pushed natural and universal principles aside. Much of the developed world, for the most part, is hardly principle centered. People have become value centered. There has been a gradual and steady degradation and erosion of true ethics and morality in the world.

Though others may emphatically disagree, I tend to think the world would be a much better place without so much competition. In business, considering what overly competitive people do to each other and those around them, teamwork has been proven to be a far better means to reach desirable ends. With extreme competition, many times in today's business world, there *is* no mercy, and people revert to uncivil methods of interacting with others. They do this while rejoicing in the self-satisfaction of *winning*, after preying upon their perceived competition. *That's just business*, as the phrase or, as I should say, the *excuse* goes. According to Lao Tzu, the father of Taoism, "*The best, like water, benefit all and do not compete...It is because they do not compete with others that they are beyond the reproach of the world.*"

Something is wrong when business tactics

and the actions of adults set ruthless examples for children. Something is wrong when teachers are ridiculed and reprimanded for effectively disciplining unruly students. Additionally, something is wrong when schools need to get parental consent to administer aspirin but don't have to inform parents of a daughter seeking an abortion. Moreover, something is wrong when kids are violently assaulted, sometimes killed, while attending public schools.

I often find it distressing how humans have become so highly technological and competitive, to the point where quality time with friends and loved ones cannot be spent due to high-tech electronic devices. It is this modern, plugged-in, accelerated type of society that is acting to rob the quality out of people's lives. We, as that society, have now set a new precedent and model for success. Consequently, educational systems are being forced to change and adapt to this new quickened and competitive world. I have witnessed this phenomenon firsthand while both teaching school as well as serving on school achievement committees. Kids attending elementary school today are increasingly exposed to an environment of highly structured, fast-paced, multitasking schedules from the minute the first bell of the day sounds, till it's time to go home. And now we're focusing on kindergarten and the preschools in much the same way. Got to get them ready for a demanding world after all.

Author, Eknath Easwaran, who taught practical spiritual skills to Western audiences for over thirty years stated, *"Under the impact of a rapidly-moving, conditioned mind, we lose our sense of freely choosing."*

It was Thoreau who told us to *simplify*, because the world was too complex. He would be astounded even more so with the world today.

I'll ask the question: Are we creating a pressure cooker where our kids are being forced to grow up too fast, instead of being allowed to simmer and season into the full flavor of principle-centered adulthood? Turn up the heat and add the pressure of broken homes, along with the associated emotional disturbances to this cooker, and you better get out of the kitchen, because we've concocted a recipe that none of us are able to stomach.

Perhaps it's time we turn the heat down and take another look at that recipe before we blow the lid off. Mass shootings, for example, represent the pressure-relief valve on the top of that cooker, and it's now frantically dancing, blowing off steam…RIBBIT.

This formula is producing a world with a high degree of incivility and insensitivity. There seems to be less professional courtesy these days, i.e., not returning important calls, letters, and messages. If people just don't want to deal with it, if it's not perceived to be important, or if they just don't like the person on the other end, for whatever reason, then simply ignore it or them, and it, or they, will hopefully go away. Brilliant! That's the type of business ethics being displayed all too often in the world today. Hardly principle centered.

Speaking of incivility, if we listed all of the bad habits that many people have (children as well as adults), which habit would you guess tops the list as being the most commonly practiced worst habit of all? Studies prove that *lying* outpaces smoking, drinking, cussing, or any other bad habit you can possibly imagine. Lying has become such a cultural norm that many people don't even think twice about their responsibility to be honest with others anymore. So-called *white lies* are still lies.

I believe society would be better served by going back to square one and teach ethics to children first, as a prerequisite to academics and getting things done quite so fast and efficient. After proper conduct becomes normal behavior, *then* introduce productivity. Character building should be the foundation of childcare as well as education – not competitive productivity aimed at materialistic values.

Some people are quick to blame our educational systems for the lack of accountability in professional learning. Granted, a primary responsibility of our schools is to educate for professional skills, however, with such a lack of character displayed in the world today, schools need to stress *ethics* in addition to academics.

Ideally, we should not have to hand that responsibility to the schools, since our educational institutions cannot begin to fill the role of parents, but many parents don't seem to be taking this responsibility all that seriously.

Grandparenting, as available, is also a fundamental form of parenting. It was my grandmother who instilled many of the concrete values and principles in me while I was growing up.

Character would be another thing that is essential. It takes character for people to be civil to each other. It takes character to deal with the challenges and adversity we face in life. Without it, there is no quality of life – only uncivil productivity and shallow materialism. Unfortunately, kids who have had their family life torn apart, and who may not have developed character, find themselves at a tremendous loss, especially in a highly competitive world.

I admit, many children are psychologically challenged from the beginning, considering those children who are born burdened by the genetics of undesirable personality traits or problems like alcohol dependency and various inherited mental illnesses. So, in fairness, we certainly can't always blame parents for child behavior. However, there are far too many kids that become mentally scarred and dysfunctional, commonly due to the level and extent of traumatic events experienced in early childhood. I would venture to guess that the majority of the problems are due to external factors and social influences, with a small amount being the result of internal factors such as inherited genetics. We know that the majority of people are not usually born dysfunctional. Like prejudice, it's a trait that is learned and acquired usually early on in life.

Humans do, however, with enough knowledge, have the ability to control this sort of behavior, as well as their prejudice, by *choice*. It's not easy, but just as it was learned and programmed into their minds, both dysfunction and prejudice may also be unlearned and deprogrammed. In that respect, the human mind works much like a computer; it's just more difficult and takes a little longer to erase certain programs and start reprograming.

As for instilled programs and personalities, it wasn't until I was given the Myers-Briggs/Keirsey-Bates Personality Test in graduate school that I finally figured out the driving forces behind our behaviors. That particular test had indicated me to be an INFJ personality type. From that, I was considered to be Introverted, iNtuitive, Feeling, and Judging. Finally, I knew what made me tick, and I could at least live with myself, even if I didn't sociologically mesh with certain people who were different from me.

Personality differences are extremely important to understand, since they often lie at the heart of human conflict, in arguments or indifferences which can lead to such things as broken relationships, divorce, abuse, and violence.

Getting to the root of instilled personalities, people become either introverted or extroverted as they grow up. Seems it's naturally about half and half, with each side contributing unique roles in society. Scientists, for example, are usually thinkers rather than talkers, and sales people are more extroverted and expressive. There are different degrees to each side, but nevertheless, once an introvert, always an introvert. The same goes for extroverts; neither one being superior to the other. I believe there has always been a natural sociological separation between the two – kind of jocks v. nerds, if you will. Whether anyone realizes, or wants to admit, this becomes a big deal in the sociology of human relations. In hindsight, we learned that this was a contributing factor that led to the violence at Columbine.

According to theories in management psychology, one cannot change their basic personality, at least not on a permanent basis. They can only learn to *choose* their behavior around their core personality. In that respect, a true introvert can learn to be more extroverted and outspoken, just as an extrovert can learn to balance an urge to talk with the skill of listening. It seems that some extroverts have a natural tendency to put down introverts for being quiet and reserved, often misperceived as a lack of personality, just as some introverts have a tendency to not respect extroverts for dominating social situations and controlling one-sided conversations.

People are commonly guilty of discriminating against others who are different from them. That's *prejudice* – be it race, creed, color, sex, or even personalities. Justly, no matter what contrariety, people are wrong to be putting others down just because they're different. Instilled principles, along with intelligence, are therefore important factors in making *wise choices* in these matters.

Unfortunately, cultural differences and the resulting discrimination that comes from them continue to be quite common in our society. As an example, I once happened to be listening to some syndicated morning talk-radio hosts putting down people who don't carry on conversations well at parties. I'm sure it was just frank radio humor, but I'm also sure that half of the people listening weren't laughing. If people would just put themselves in the shoes of others that they may so openly criticize, even in humor, they might develop a different perspective and not be so quick to prejudge and discriminate. If everyone could develop this knowledge, we would quickly eliminate much of the conflict and violence that exists in the world.

I can empathize with people who haven't

learned healthy confrontation techniques in order to contend in this fast-paced and insensitive world. With young people, it can lead to *bullying* and, God forbid, situations like Columbine. With adults, it may actually evolve into mental states such as Social Anxiety Disorder (SAD) estimated to affect approximately ten percent of the population. Society has a bad habit of discriminating against people inflicted with these disorders, which only intensifies the problem. These mental conditions likely come from traumatic experiences in childhood associated with abuse, rejection, and abandonment and may even be hereditary.

Generally, it's safe to say that most of the so-called popular people, young or old, found in the world are outgoing and don't suffer as much from the results of rejection and abandonment as others do. Further, as shallow as it may sound, studies on popularity indicate that males are most valued being tall and athletic, while females are primarily appreciated for their looks and the way they dress. Okay, so I just described Ken and Barbie. In any case, it's obviously a disadvantage to be the opposite of these popular traits in a highly competitive, *value*-centered, rather than *principle*-centered world. Again, it's extremely important to note that these influences on kids have a great effect on how their personalities develop.

Early influences are huge. I can remember growing up in a small town with a grandmother who knew practically everyone on a first-name basis. Additionally, my mother had been raised with some of the people who were now my teachers. Looking back, I feel quite fortunate living in that influential and secure environment. The only disadvantage was having a broken home with a missing father.

Even though I came from a broken home, split families weren't quite so prevalent in the 1960s, as they are now. According to the figures taken from a recent census, only three out of five children were living with both parents in the same household. That says that 40 percent of kids are living in broken homes. Thankfully, in my case, I turned out mostly okay, but I could have easily gone down another path in a less positively influential and unsecured environment.

In retrospect of my own childhood, even though we kids may have been less than perfect, we were taught respect for authority. If I had shown any disrespect toward adults, teachers, or the law, well, that strictly wasn't tolerated. In those days, principle-centered kids never thought about planning and instigating any type of violence, especially not at school. We were taught better than that.

Related to the social challenges of growing up, an article that I once read talked about our super-mobile, hyper-connected, multitasking, media-saturated society where tension is a serious and growing concern. It said that more and more children are diagnosed with attention-deficit hyperactivity disorder (ADHD), and that many adults, increasingly, are displaying symptoms of it as well. And, of course, the pharmaceutical companies have drugs for it.

ADHD is a term in psychiatry that refers to a condition where people simply don't or can't pay attention to what's going on around them. In that respect, it can also greatly affect reading comprehension. Many people diagnosed with ADHD coincidentally happen to be a little high strung, probably due to the level of constant stress in their lives. Perhaps people just can't focus their attention anymore due to all the distractions in today's world. Maybe they're just hyperactive because that's how their brains naturally cope with information overload and stress. When you think about the magnitude of information that the modern human brain has to decipher each day, it's easy to understand how it can become overloaded trying to process it all. Don't put me in a multitasking situation all day long, where I have to do six things at once, plus answer a phone that won't stop ringing. I don't think extreme multitasking is either physically or mentally healthy.

A recipe for early emotional problems and delinquency in kids is to add a busy, crazy, unethical world, and abruptly remove at least one parent. These mixed-up youth, added in with other mixed-up children, along with media filled with sex and graphic violence, can be emotionally disturbing. Now put these kids in a social environment that removes all confidence and self-esteem. For a spicier recipe, wait for puberty, add cigarettes, alcohol, and drugs. Then serve with the counselor and pharmaceutical of your choice.

Sadly, playground politics carries into adult life, and as everyone knows, bullying is a huge problem no matter what age. Personally, I had my share of playground fights with bullies. I can remember having to go to the school nurse to have the gravel picked out of my knees and elbows, and then to the principal's office to have the stupidity picked out of my head, and a paddle put to my butt. That's back when school principals still carried paddle permits and when children were held accountable for their actions. Kids today are given too many adult rights when they need to be held accountable and take responsibility for their actions.

Outside of that principal's office, we boys never seemed to have any problem creating and inventing our own forms of entertainment – some of it constructive, some of it not. Today, I see more and more boys being less and less constructive and more destructive, and sometimes violent.

In my day, boys would build kites, model airplanes, and tree houses as daytime activities. Summer nights were spent just camping out in the backyard, staring at the stars, while contemplating the vastness of the universe, and maybe where the Little Dipper was. Young boys rarely paid much attention to girls. Today, kids are exposed to explicit sexual content at a very early age with all the *sex sells* media. Consequently, they are starting to actually *have* sex at ages when they used to think twice about just kissing.

What we're doing today is programming kids' minds, and the programmed mind is a very powerful thing and sometimes dangerous to have to deal with, especially when the programs become infected and go bad.

The environment where a kid grows up is critical to the adult he or she becomes. For me, I think growing up in a small town in rural Colorado was one of the best things that ever happened to me. I pity the kids today that have to grow up in inner cities. I think rural life is somewhat better for raising children, but people don't always have that choice in this modern age.

Growing up in rural areas, kids often spend most of their formative years in the great outdoors working and recreating, like doing chores first thing in the morning, then hiking, biking, camping, fishing, and having lots of good, clean fun.

Recreation and work have always been good ways for kids to burn off excess energy, and a means to keep them out of trouble as well as their parents' hair. That's possibly one of the reasons I initially made my career in the recreation industry. Recreational activities are far more productive and less destructive than spray painting graffiti on public property. Not that we never did anything like that, but Graffiti, along with defacing and destroying public property, has since gotten way out of hand. It seems many kids today have little to no respect for the property of others.

In the past, Scouting was another great experience for kids, especially for the ones who didn't have fathers. Scouting did a lot for my character. There's no better way for kids to get in touch with nature, science, civics, or themselves. However, with today's social conflicts, the future of Scouting is in jeopardy.

In the past, Scouting always had a way of teaching kids profound lessons in life. I remember one time when our Cub Scout Pack was giving a Christmas performance at the local town hall. We were all made up to look like Indians for this particular performance. This included not only wearing Indian costumes, but we were to put a brownish red cosmetic substance all over our bodies in order to look the part. As fate would have it, I was the only light-complexioned kid in our entire Cub Scout Pack that was allergic to that stuff, so I consequently was the only one not wearing it that night. There I was, dressed in Indian attire just like all the other kids on that stage, but there was obviously something very different about me. I soon found out what it was like to be the only different kid on the block. That experience became my first lesson in diversity. It taught me what it actually feels like to be a minority in this world – a principle I would never forget.

For thousands of years, the nations and people of the world have been at war with each other, simply because the other was physically, politically, or religiously different. Prejudice is an extremely powerful and evil force that many people continue to practice and teach their kids.

The fact that we, as imperfect humans, are still prejudiced toward people different from ourselves has contributed to society's incapability of justly managing itself. How many more political, religious, or racial wars is it going to take before we finally find true peace in the world?

In principle, spiritual faith can be a good thing for children. The summer religious retreats that I attended as a boy were spiritually moving and joyful experiences. Looking back, I can honestly say that I would not trade those experiences for the chance to attend the Super Bowl if offered to me. Sadly, I fear that a lot of people today would opt for the Super Bowl if given the choice. Did you know that nearly half of Americans now faithfully watch the Super Bowl each year? Do you think that you could ever get half of America to be spiritually faithful?

Who can deny that people have become

much more materialistic than spiritual? Just look at halftime commercials.

Personally, I may not spend much time in church anymore, since I don't completely agree with the philosophies of any one religion, but I still believe in a higher power and consider myself to be spiritual in that regard. Ultimately, I feel church resides in people's hearts, in the way they live, act, and relate to others, and not necessarily under any religious doctrine.

There is separation of church and state, and there is separation of media and reality. I remember, as a young boy, watching guys like the Lone Ranger, Marshal Dillon, and the Rifleman save the day. They were our heroes. Little did we accept the fact that they were only performers acting out parts. Today, like the song, we might ask ourselves, *where have all the cowboys gone?* They're around. But, as usual, they're not always found at the movies or in sports arenas. If kids want to see cowboys (heroes), they only need to look around their own realities, such as emergency responders.

Too many people are looking for cowboys and heroes in all the wrong places. Entertainers and athletes are not necessarily heroes – they're all too often merely celebrities *pretending* to be heroes.

As for *real* heroes, they can be found at fire and police stations across the land, as well as behind the wheel of ambulances, in hospital emergency rooms, and at disaster shelters. Additionally, our public schools contain more than a few knights in shining armor too, like the school teacher shot to death while heroically shielding his students from the terror at Columbine High.

Yes, our public service professionals are the real heroes. Tell me who the heroes were on September 11, 2001. Furthermore, it's assuring to know that they're always there for us and always will be, and that they're obviously not in it for the money. Moreover, with the way the world is headed, I'm afraid we'll only come to depend on them more and more in the future.

Unfortunately, there's not as much glamour or pay in being a public servant as there is in being a movie or sports celebrity. The teacher and police shortage we're experiencing would support that. In the past, as well as today, teachers and public service professionals have always been there for kids. For example, in the early 1960s, I couldn't begin to fully understand the implications, but I remember having to go through all the drills at school where we had to crouch under our desks with our arms folded over our heads. That's when the cold war between the United States and the Soviet Union was at its peak with all of the ominous nuclear deployments going on. Our teachers guided and assured us through all these drills and troubled times. Because of them, we were never very concerned or all that scared. I think our teachers were probably a little frightened, but they rarely displayed their fear in front of their classes.

So, how would people ever get by without the dedicated public servants and emergency professionals that are summoned by simply dialing 911 from any telephone?

Where have all the cowboys gone? The truth is, they haven't gone anywhere, nor are they going anywhere in the future. They'll always be there for us – the ones that kids can truly depend on and can continue to look up to.

Ah, the formative years. Outside of a few bad days that came with the territory, as I remember, life was good. I guess I'd have to say that those times, even with their downfalls, were, for the most part, the best years of our lives, locked fondly and securely into our memories.

Those were the days of true freedom, of catching pigeons, frogs, and garden snakes, netting butterflies and capturing bees and bugs in jars, climbing trees, lying around in the grass, and jumping into piles of fallen leaves. They were the days of eating a sour green apple that you had just picked, building forts, digging up worms, and catching night crawlers. The days of gardening and helping to preserve the harvest, hunting, fishing, and foraging from the land. They were the days of playing in the snow, sledding, ice skating, and building igloos till we could hardly feel our fingers and toes. In short, those times offered the sheer excitement of exploring while experiencing and trying to understand the natural world around us – perhaps indirectly helping to prepare us for adulthood and the real world that lay ahead. There were valuable principles and lessons of managing life to learn.

Why is it that for many of us, after we've passed our childhood era, we often, at least in the back of our minds, wish we could escape adulthood to go back to relive those innocent, formative, and natural years? Perhaps it's because it was the last time in our lives that we found ourselves in perfect harmony with nature and each other. Or, it might also have simply been the last time that we experienced an authentic level of complete excitement over relatively simple things in life.

Something oddly predictable happens after that formative phase of youth; kids start to grow up and often become preoccupied with all the wrong things, and for all the wrong reasons.

Dawning Puberty

Roll with the Changes
— REO Speedwagon

As pointed out in the last two chapters, life, for the most part, is fairly innocent and basically uncomplicated during our childhood and formative years, that is, until the hormones start to kick in.

Like a tadpole becoming a frog, the human body starts to change as we leave childhood and approach our adolescent years. Naturally preparing itself for reproduction, the body experiences an onset of biological chemicals that not only affects the physical being, but also drastically affects our mental reasoning abilities as well. These hormones are extremely potent and powerful natural chemical substances.

I can remember hitting that wall of puberty and my older brother setting me straight over the dinner table one evening for talking back to my mother. At the time, I probably didn't mean what was coming out of my mouth, but like a science fiction movie, where creatures from outer space invade and take over human bodies, I was under the influence of alien hormones.

With effective discipline still at the helm of parenting back in the 1950s and 1960s when I was growing up, many kids assuredly received a verbal tongue-lashing from adults in reciprocation for their newfound cockiness. A few less-fortunate boys might have even found themselves out behind the woodshed for giving their dads that kind of disrespectful lip service. That was a time when most parents not only commanded respect but usually deserved it as well. Many kids today don't seem to respect adults much. Could it be that adults have to earn respect from children, just as bosses have to earn respect from employees, and much the same way that politicians have to earn respect from their constituents? It's not hard to see why leadership is losing ground in the world today.

Young people still experience the same transitions and transformations that we adults did at their age, but some things, like obedience, have certainly changed. A major problem, as I see it, is that kids too often are not being taught self-discipline. Without mastering the art of self-restraint, people stand to mismanage and lose control of their lives. Furthermore, related to teaching discipline, too many parents are not taking responsibility for the whereabouts and actions of their children, with the result that kids often get into trouble. With enough instilled self-discipline, kids know better how to abstain from temptations, overrule peer pressures, and avoid trouble.

With old-school disciplinary measures,

spankings, considered a form of violence anymore, though they may have been effective in the short term at an early age, are becoming obsolete, since they lead to resentment and don't actually teach children how to modify their behavior. On the other hand, kids today are being given far too many rights and freedoms before they're emotionally capable or sufficiently responsible to handle them. And with our current legal systems, parents and/or teachers can't so much as lay a hand on kids, leaving the slightest mark, either in punishment or love, without social services stepping in to evaluate the child's environment for domestic abuse. In their defense, we should give social services credit, since they have an almost impossible job to do. Many times, they're damned if they do and damned if they don't. I know of one instance where a girl told her teacher that she was being abused at home, in order to get even with her mother for refusing her permission to wear trendy, worn-out jeans full of holes. In that particular situation, while there may have been extenuating circumstances involved, social services separated the girl from her mother for a mandated period of time and placed her in a foster home. Out of spite, kids have also been known to pull these same types of cheap tricks on their teachers, getting them in trouble with the school administration and authorities. Many parents and teachers are slowly losing not only power, but also respect from the kids they technically and legally oversee.

Here's a basic principle of managing children as well as a reliable parenting and teaching strategy: *The parents and teachers should be the ones in charge – not the kids*. The problem is you can't take charge of anyone without their respect *for* you or their fear *of* you. Provided there *is* some respect, *because I said so* may be old fashioned, but it still works.

If kids are raised correctly with proper values and principles, they'd rarely think of doing disrespectful things to their parents, their teachers, *or* their peers. Disrespect too often comes in the form of violence. Such was the case at Columbine High.

In the words of one of the all-time premier actors and producers, Denzel Washington, who said, "*We live in a society where 12 and 14-year-old boys beat their father to death with a baseball bat. Anger is a real problem right now, and there is something going on in this country that's making young people explode*." He went on to say, "*You can't legislate love. We got the biggest government in the world and we got fourteen-year-olds murdering kids in cold blood. So, obviously, more government, more legislation isn't the answer. It starts in the home*." He profoundly added, "*Like my mother used to say, by the time you're six years old, if the parents haven't instilled certain things, it's too late. The government and society can give us tools to work with as parents and protect children's and parents' rights, but it starts in the family.*"

According to the American Academy of Child and Adolescent Psychiatry (AACAP), numerous research studies have concluded that a complex interaction or combination of factors lead to an increased risk of violent behavior in children and adolescents.

These factors include:

- Previous aggressive or violent behavior.
- Being the victim of physical abuse and/or sexual abuse.
- Exposure to violence in the home and/or community.
- Genetic (family heredity) factors.
- Exposure to violence in media (TV, movies, video and computer games, etc.).
- Use of drugs and/or alcohol.
- Presence of firearms in the home.
- The combination of stressful family socioeconomic factors (poverty, severe deprivation, marital breakup, single parenting, unemployment, loss of support from extended family).
- Brain damage from head injury.

The AACAP also indicated that these research studies have shown that violent behavior can be decreased or even prevented if the above risk factors are significantly reduced or eliminated. Clearly, claims the academy,

Violence leads to violence. In addition, the following strategies can lessen or prevent violent behavior:

- Prevention of child abuse (use of programs such as parent training, family support programs, etc.).
- Sex education and parenting programs for adolescents.
- Early intervention programs for violent youngsters.
- Monitoring child's viewing of violence on TV/videos/movies.

It's known that the perpetrators at Columbine High were often exposed to violent forms of media.

It all comes down to proactive education and prevention – teaching values, principles, and ethics, rather than reactive legal and/or punitive actions that inevitably result in damaged or destroyed relationships. Leaders, however, have to walk their talk. Set bad examples, and you instantly forfeit the game. Discipline kids without modeled behavior or justified respect, and you've just created a kid that will only resent and perhaps hate you for it.

Concerning discipline outside of the home, such as at school, some parents are too quick to run to the defense of their kids while thinking; *How dare anyone discipline or punish my child!* Fortunately, most parents aren't like that and will investigate the situation further before jumping to conclusions. However, there are a growing number of parents that sharply criticize the schools as well as the teachers before knowing all the facts. Oftentimes the children involved will sit back and gloat because they won against the establishment, making the establishment even less effective than it already is. And we wonder why public education is faltering.

Often, though, it takes more than discipline or punishment. Strict discipline alone won't solve the problem and is only one important part of raising children. With some kids, we're often too late to correct their undesirable behaviors. The troubled kids I'm referring to need positive influences in their lives, plus genuine love and respect. For them, the window of opportunity for correcting their behavior may be quickly closing.

According to Jeff Jacoby of the Boston Globe, who wrote; *"It wasn't the case that the parents of John Walker Lindh (the Marin County child of privilege turned Taliban terrorist) never drew the line with their son. True, they didn't do so when he was fourteen and his consuming passion was collecting hip-hop CDs with especially nasty lyrics. And true, they didn't put their foot down when he announced at sixteen that he was going to drop out of Tamiscal High School (the elite alternative school where students determined their own course of study and saw a teacher only once a week). And granted they didn't interfere when he abruptly decided to become a Muslim after reading the Autobiography of Malcolm X, grew a beard, and took to wearing long white robes and an oversized skullcap.*" Jacoby pointed out that John Walker Lindh's father was *"proud of his son for pursuing an alternative course"*, and that his mother told friends that it was *"good for a child to find a passion."* When *Newsweek* called it *"truly perplexing"* that John Walker Lindh, *"who grew up in possibly the most liberal, tolerant place in America, while being drawn to the most illiberal, intolerant sect in Islam"*, Jacoby countered, *"Even in Marin County, there are times when children need to hear No and Don't."* He went on to say, *"They need to know that there are limits they must respect and expectations they must try to live up to. If they cannot find those limits and expectations at home, they are apt to look for them elsewhere. There is nothing perplexing about it. He* (meaning John Walker Lindh) *craved standards and discipline. Mom and Dad didn't offer any – the Taliban did. Even when it was clear that their son was sinking into Islamist fanaticism, they wouldn't pull back on the reins. But his road to treason and jihad didn't begin in Afghanistan. It began in Marin County, with parents who never said No."*

The mother of an old friend of mine, who had spent many years working with emotionally disturbed kids, wrote her daughter the following comment on Jacoby's article, saying, *"This is a conservative viewpoint on what brought John*

Walker Lindh to the place he is today. It is a sad commentary on many young people and parents in America. Those of us who have spent our careers working with emotionally disturbed students can see our students and their families in this report."

Again, it needs to be reiterated that even though discipline is crucial in the whole process, strict discipline alone, no matter what the situation, is no panacea for raising good kids. Without genuine love and modeled behavior, it only breeds resentment and rebellion. Likewise, no discipline at all, as in the case of John Walker Lindh, can also turn out to be a disaster.

Quality principle-centered parenting, while respecting a child's individuality, also requires setting boundaries. Additionally, it involves assisting children to achieve their potential, while helping them learn to make *wise choices.*

Taking these responsibilities as a parent is essential to raising stable children. Discipline merely becomes the mortar between the bricks of that foundation. Too many people are having kids without even thinking about the inherent responsibilities of this commitment.

According to Dr. Laura Schlessinger, from her best-selling book *Stupid Things Parents Do to Mess up Their Kids*, she indicates, "*In our society, reproductive freedom means anyone can decide to create a life by any means with no, and I mean no, consideration of what is in the best interest of that new human being.*" She went on to say, "*The cavalier manner in which our society treats child care, not as a matter of intimacy and love, but as a matter of convenience and economics, is deeply destructive to our children's sense of attachment, identity, and importance.*"

Ironically, many people have rashly and straightforwardly criticized Dr. Laura for being so rash and straightforward, to which I would say, they should learn how to take constructive criticism.

Too many people are not taking family commitments seriously. In the case of separation and divorce, to bail out of a family relationship at the expense of your kids, just for your own personal convenience, is not only selfish, but also *childish* in itself. In that situation, you surely stand to destroy other innocent lives in addition to your own.

My viewpoints on quality parenting and family leadership may not come from experience as a parent but from an important and critical set of principles for organizational development and leadership – a subject matter in which I do have expertise. In that respect, a family, most assuredly, is an organization, as much as any business or corporation. The relational dynamics between the organizational members are virtually the same.

Leadership, therefore, in any kind of organization, including families, is a combination of genuine care and affection, combined with ethical discipline, along with taking responsibility for the sake of the organization over the long haul. In companies, corporations, and other organizations, discipline alone, without genuine care for the internal stakeholders, can be described as autocratic, uncaring management, which is an obsolete form of leadership that is surprisingly still used today in many organizations, including families as well as entire countries.

Similarly with families, discipline alone, without the rest of the formula, is nothing short of abuse, be it mental or physical. And yes, there are abusive parents out there, but that's a whole other sociological problem in itself that we won't dwell upon here.

On the other hand, I believe that some of the punitive legal constraints dealing with child discipline, be it at home or at school, mental or physical, are ultimately hurting our society. Looking at it from a systems management perspective, the entire situation has started to snowball and, as we've been experiencing, will only get worse before it gets better, that is, unless we as a society take action to make changes.

There is absolutely nothing wrong with disciplining a child for good reason, as long as it remains non-abusive. Conversely, kids hiring lawyers and suing their parents should not be happening, but that situation has been occurring.

Fame and fortune, in more than one case, has led popular child stars to sue their own parents. If parents and their children can't work out their personal disagreements without lawyers entering the picture, then I'm afraid the world has a big problem. Children, regardless of the circumstances, provided parents are being responsible, should respect their parent enough to negotiate a solution to their problems.

As with all family legal disputes, these situations do nothing but irreparably destroy fragile relationships. These families may need psychological counselors more than legal ones.

Working as a substitute teacher in the public-school systems, I was often exposed to the full onslaught of ill dispositions and disrespect for adults. Sure, we used to do disrespectful things to substitute teachers in my day too, but it's since gotten far worse and much more of a common cultural normality than it used to be.

Mannerisms seem to be getting steadily worse throughout the world. Other societies have always had problems dealing with the inadequacies of instilled manners too. In fact, Thoreau noticed this selfish human tendency when he wrote, "*Nations are possessed with an insane ambition to perpetuate the memory of themselves by the amount of hammered stone they leave. What if equal pains were taken to smooth and polish their manners?*" Could he have been referring to the Roman Empire, in part, when he wrote that? I think we all know where *their* declining manners got *them*.

As a teacher, I had to supervise weightlifting classes containing several cocky boys that can't seem to complete their workout unless they're listening to loud mean-sounding rap, so-called music, repetitively emanating four-letter words per whatever you care to call them, songs? In those situations, I usually just turned the stereo off, while explaining to the class that I personally don't appreciate that kind of nauseating, negative noise in a class for which I'm responsible. Incidentally, I was usually considered a *jerk* for doing that...so sue me.

We think we have a problem in the world with ingested drugs and alcohol. I'm here to tell you that the most dangerous natural drug, produced by Mother Nature, mostly associated with the emergence of puberty, is the male biological hormone *testosterone*.

Testosterone is the most common representative of the male sex hormones collectively called androgens. Using cholesterol as a base, on average, the male gonads (testes) produce between four and ten milligrams of testosterone per day, having a dominating effect on both physical and mental processes. Following puberty, testosterone levels are at their lifetime peak, and they don't begin to decline until around the age of twenty-three.

Female hormones, like estrogen and

progesterone, while being quite powerful and mood altering themselves, generally produce relatively less aggressive traits among women, compared to male hormones.

Additionally, a number of athletes and jocks are taking supplemental hormones, which act only to make them *especially* strong and aggressive. That may be a good thing out on the football field for their own team, but it consequently is neither needed nor appreciated on the streets of our cities and in the hallways of our schools.

Testosterone has undeniably and directly contributed to senseless violence throughout human history. Be it gang problems, terrorism, and nonsensical violent eruptions, including road rage, they are the direct result of irresponsible actions usually brought about by young men in their hormonal crests.

Since we, as a society, can't remove nature's hormones from the picture, what *can* we do? There is something that can help to offset the mood-altering effects of these chemicals – teaching ethics and self-discipline. The best thing society can do is to go back to square one and teach good values and principles to these kids, through proper parenting and education, so that they make *wise choices* later on in life. After all, there has to be a point where intelligence takes over for cocky stupidity. It takes good judgment to overcome the urge to be violent, or to turn the other cheek. Young men who surround themselves with violence and terror obviously have not reached that level of intelligence and wisdom.

Some may argue that certain girls are capable of causing problems too. Sure, there are some over-saucy, even brainwashed females in the world, but predominantly, due to testosterone, the male gender, regarding aggressive behavior, presents the biggest problems. After all, *boys will be boys* is a phrase heard far more often than *girls will be girls*.

Outside of terrorists and other unethical gangs, the widespread problems that young cocky males cause are prevalent everywhere you look. For example, in the summer of 1999, the second Woodstock concert was held on the thirtieth-year anniversary of the original concert, which took place in the summer of 1969, during the Vietnam War era. Apparently, there was a riot that unfolded at the more recent event, resulting in many injuries. The news reports we heard referred to what they called *macho idiots* that started the whole thing. The reports didn't specifically say, but I'm sure they were referring to males when they said *macho*, since both genders were probably present, and both genders, as we well know, are perfectly capable of being idiots.

How ironic for these so-called macho idiots to stage war and to become violent at a concert with a historical theme based on peace, love, and ending war and violence. No doubt drugs and alcohol were involved in the situation, but I would also venture to guess that these boys were also under the influence of a certain hormone at the time.

These kinds of violent situations always make the news, since we're all somewhat interested in them, but, like frogs in hot water, we've developed a tendency to mostly ignore our changing environment. We've become immune and callous to being shocked and appalled, especially if we happen to be the police or the attorneys involved.

Unfortunately, the machismo ego has a tendency to outweigh common decency in our current society in many cases, such as in aggressive contact sports. Take football and hockey for example. Outside of the *official* rules of football, it's perfectly acceptable for a right tackle to physically cream a quarterback or for a hockey player to accidentally put his stick across the face of his opponent, even if it means sitting in hockey jail – *five for fighting*, as they call it. In fact, that's just part of the game, and if it weren't, no one else with any hormones themselves would pay good money to watch. Didn't the Romans have the same type of culture before their civilization fell apart? I think they were called *Gladiators* back then instead of *Raiders*. Today's level of ethics in sports, as well as the media, becomes a challenge.

I could spend the rest of this book describing one dysfunctional situation after another going on out there, but I think we all get the point. They're just everyday situations with everyday people – hundreds, maybe even thousands of them, a day. A great deal of them being the indirect result of cocky mentalities multiplied by the inability to make *wise choices*.

Again, we need to go to the root of the problem early on, back to the home as well as the classroom, and learn how to control these outbursts of anger and violence through a process of instilled ethics and self-discipline.

As I remember growing up, with the onset of puberty, we boys would eye practically any and every type of pretty, female-focused media we could get our hands on. The scores of risqué magazines on the bookshelves of today didn't exist. However, with today's media, including the Internet, things have advanced considerably since those days. Accessibility to pornography is now a twenty-four-hour playground, furthering the obstacles to instilling decent principles in kids. With so much pornography easily available today, boys soon grow impatient with just looking, which, even at an early age, commonly now leads to actual sex.

It's uncanny how children, while growing up, are influenced by parents and other adults. I can remember one of the boys I grew up with, who went on to become the head of a large company that merged with another big corporation, making him worth hundreds of millions of dollars. Being raised in the same small town together, I can also remember a time when I bought a squeeze-horn that mounted on the front handlebars of my bicycle. Shortly afterward, this particular boy came riding up to me on *his* bike, making a real scene for me to pull over. He then proceeded to *bully* me over what he indirectly, in not so many words, referred to as violating copyrights with the horn on my bike, and instructed me to remove it because he had one just like it on *his* bike. His reasoning was that he had the exclusive rights within the neighborhood to the handlebar squeeze-horn, explaining that when other kids heard it, they would immediately know it was *him* coming. Gee, I wonder where kids get this sort of egotistical behavior, if not from their parents and other adults. Incidentally, this boy's father happened to be a big-shot businessman, which may have had something to do with it.

According to Cameroonian proverb, *Knowledge is better than riches.* I once had the opportunity, while serving on the local school district achievement accountability advisory committee, to ask any education-related question I desired to a panel of young people made up of a mixture of secondary (middle and high school) students. I asked them, *"If you had the choice, which would you choose – knowledge without wealth or wealth without knowledge, and why?"* All of these kids, with the exception of one boy, chose knowledge over wealth. The most common reason offered was that with enough knowledge, one can achieve anything, including wealth, if one so chooses, but we cannot buy knowledge. Today's kids are fairly savvy in that respect.

It's hard to explain the power girls suddenly possess over boys after puberty. Once this event occurs, young women seem to sense it, and a new political skirmish starts to unfold. Unfortunately, this contention slowly but surely develops into a full-fledged power struggle between the genders. Girls growing into attractive women begin to recognize that they possess a valuable commodity that men want. Blessed with this resource that more than makes up for the lack of physical size and strength inherent to the male gender, women come to realize that the deck is actually stacked in *their* favor. Consequently, sex has become a primary influence in our society. Sex, along with money, as primary values in modern society, has much to do with the direction in which the world is currently headed.

As for money, it used to be, for the most part, earned by men. However, money is now being more equitably earned by both genders, even though men sometimes still make more for doing the same job, but the last figures I read indicated that one in three women in the United States now earn more money than their husbands. When you consider the power of sex and money together, some women are quickly reaching and, in some cases, exceeding the equal rights they bargained for.

As an important, relevant issue and disadvantage of society, both genders competing with each other for jobs eventually ended the ability of one spouse to bring home enough money for the entire family's subsistence, thereby causing the average wage to drop relative to the cost of living. Today, even though one spouse may make more than the other, it's common for both spouses to need to work in order to make ends meet. All this did was give more productivity, profits, and power to big businesses and totally disrupted the family order. With mom and dad now both chained to the working world, it also created a bunch of latchkey kids. I'll leave it to your imagination the unsupervised trouble *they* can get into.

As a prime example of the challenge that families now face, even with both parents working, just look at the housing crisis that has unfolded. According to *USA Today*, home prices have jumped so high in the United States that even middle-class families are challenged to find affordable housing while having to devote more of their income to that. The skyrocketing costs of housing have pushed many potential new buyers out of the market. The problem has become so bad that experts say housing affordability has reached *crisis* levels in many areas of the country. To support this reasoning, *USA Today* also indicated that family income has trailed the rise in home prices, even though the number of dual-income households has increased. The article explained that a quarter of all homeowners and four in ten renters spend at least 30 percent of their income on housing, according to Harvard University's Joint Center for Housing Studies. It was noted that mortgage companies generally believe that 30 percent of income is the limit on homeowner or renter affordability. Anyone above that is considered vulnerable, especially if one person in a dual-income family loses his or her job. In the resort areas where I've worked, employees often have to devote at least half of their income to housing.

I'm afraid we created a real dilemma in childrearing when both parents were forced into the working world. What is it that was really gained? The ability to make more money? Obviously, the more money families make, the higher the cost of living. Supply and demand, along with inflation, will always dictate that.

Was it really meaningful and important enough, in principle, for humans to neglect natural child-rearing roles and responsibilities, or to turn kids over to others to raise? In retrospect, was it worth losing family values? How many parents are there who feel guilty near the end of the workday, knowing in their hearts that they should be home to greet their kids at the door after school? Don't misinterpret me, I'm not saying that both parents shouldn't seek professional careers, but look at what it is doing to families. What I'm saying is that it is seldom to a family's advantage for both parents to attempt to juggle careers and family at the same time. Whenever we do that, children and family values will often suffer sociological consequences.

Unfortunately, sex, careers, and money have now become more valuable than household relationships and responsibilities. With women controlling the power struggle over sex and quickly gaining in careers and money, where does that leave the family *as a value*? The skyrocketing divorce rate is starting to make sense.

I would propose that as intelligent human beings entering a new era, it's about time we all dropped the false values and start to openly and honestly discuss social realities. We have to do this before we can ever hope to repair and improve our way of life. If it's broken, then let's take the time and the responsibility to fix it. We should stop sweeping it under the rug for the next generation to trip over. After all, it seems that everyone entering relationships and professions these days say that they're *sick and tired of all the game playing.* So, I say, let's all *quit* playing games and start functionally and effectively communicating and interacting with each other. Sure, sometimes the truth hurts, but it can never hurt nearly as much as the opposing deceit and dishonesty associated with the games people play.

So, here's another principle of managing life: *True love and respect, in any situation or relationship, cannot exist until both sides lay down their power, wholeheartedly, while genuinely and completely surrendering to each other.* That's where true-family and good-neighbor policies begin and end.

This concept becomes a universal principle of all human relationships. However, the challenge is actually putting it into practice. That takes total trust and commitment. As a rule, you can't have love until you establish genuine trust, and there can't be trust until there is truth and honesty, which ultimately requires instilled ethics. Therefore, truth and honesty are the foundation of trust, which together become the basis of love and respect for one another. It simply, in principle, does not and cannot work any other way.

All in all, puberty, along with all of the political situations that follow it, becomes a real turning point, if not a stumbling block, in our lives. Kids can suddenly find themselves sailing into uncharted and rougher waters, compared to the ones previously navigated. Without unyielding values and principles, children may never experience the true joy and love of genuine family – only the lust of sex, careers and money, and the heartache of broken relationships.

The process of growing up without *wise choices* being made can be a real challenge, if not a disaster.

Troubled Teens

Bridge Over Troubled Water

— **Paul Simon**

All too often, troubled teens grow up to become troubled adults. The root problem, many times, has something to do with the way they were raised.

Surveys and studies on the morality of American adolescents indicate that nearly half lie to their parents and teachers, cheat on tests, and drink alcohol. In fact, about a quarter of the alcohol consumed in the United States is by underage teenagers, with about a third of teens found to binge-drink at least once a week.

Furthermore, youth violence and suicide have reached epidemic proportions creating a national crisis.

Many teens have admitted to skipping school for fear of being bullied by other kids, and one out of four will be confronted with a gun or a knife before becoming an adult. I wouldn't want to be a teenager in today's world, though I did have a knife pulled on me back when I was a teen.

With approximately 10% of 17 million high school students in America attempting suicide each year, something has drastically gone wrong with the morality and social structure of our society.

Considering three out of four emotionally disturbed teens that commit suicide come from broken homes, what would you say is the root cause of teen suicide? If you said broken homes, you're on the right track but not digging deep enough. In order to get to the root of things, we might want to look at recent history.

Corporate consolidation, due to the industrial and technological revolutions, has had a tendency to concentrate most of the increasing population in urban areas and has brought about a whole spectrum of highly challenging social problems as a result. Reality dictates that social problems have a tendency to increase proportionately with the increasing population.

Outside of highly populated cities, rural farming and ranching, which had always been a primary industry due to product demand, has now become just another big business. Due to mergers and acquisitions in recent years, most American grain exports are under the direct control of just a few large corporations. One of the adverse effects of this corporate consolidation is the steady acquisition of small farms and ranches across the heartland of America.

Many families that once ran these farms and ranches have slowly but surely been displaced. I can't help but to think that this situation has directly contributed to our current rise in social problems and that the shift in population from rural farming and ranching to urban industries has greatly influenced the downfall of family structure. Consequently, I believe this overall trend has had a substantial effect on the divorce rate and the number of broken homes we're now experiencing. Why? As mentioned, the corporate world slowly but surely forced both parents to have to leave home each day for the sake of making a living. With farming and ranching, work for the whole family, including the kids, *was* at home, and families that work together, stay together for the most part.

With modern life and broken homes, due to the unavailability and the lack of leadership of both parents, the culture among teens is becoming much less family oriented and consequently more troubled than that of previous generations. You can't keep them down on the farm and off the streets when the family farm is no longer there for them.

As a teenager, I was also uprooted out of the country and transplanted into an urban setting. It wasn't long before I found myself running around with the wrong crowd, sneaking alcohol from our parents, smoking cigarettes, using foul language, and getting into all sorts of trouble in and out of school. At one point, I was lucky I wasn't enrolled at a local reform school, but due to my foundation of ethics and my fear of reform schools, I *wisely chose* another route of going straight and keeping my nose clean. My sister, who was also miserable with our living situation, became pregnant, leaving home and getting married at the premature age of sixteen.

With all the domestic pressures at home and the social pressures at school, I can honestly recall having thoughts of suicide at one point. Again, the main thing that kept me from it was the deep-seated amount of character that had been instilled in me at an early age. Those character traits caused me to ultimately make the right, *wise choice*. I realized that committing suicide was nothing short of irresponsible and would stand to only hurt others.

Now, we should reconsider the root problem of teen suicide. As I indicated, in my mind, it's not from finding oneself living in the city in a broken home. Outside of a small percentage of genetically inherited mental illnesses, I strongly believe suicide is caused by a lack of deeply instilled values and principles, which can lead to a lack of character, confidence, and self-esteem. In many teen suicide cases, broken homes and adverse living situations are merely the final straw when one's integrity is not strong enough for one to hold on. And with parents being so busy, teens often feel that no one cares.

With many troubled youths, even though their gut feelings and consciences may be telling them that what they are doing is wrong, as I experienced myself, peer pressure often overrules moral reluctance in the matter. Things like cigarettes, alcohol, despicable media, and foul language tend to become a common crutch. Some kids, depending on their vulnerability, often find perceived safety and security within groups of similar kids (gangs), which become surrogate families, so to speak.

After getting into my share of trouble and getting caught, by the age of fifteen, I did manage to change for the better. I quit wasting my life and got a job. Additionally, I entered the highly disciplined auxiliary of the United States Air Force, the Civil Air Patrol, as a cadet, which did wonders to keep me out of any further trouble. All *wise choices*.

A primary principle of management that was reinforced to me in graduate school would be that *crisis causes change*. Hopefully, with troubled youth, change is positive rather than negative. Unfortunately, there are times when values and principles become overshadowed by deep emotional disturbance that can lead to anger and violence.

Case in point, and what started me writing this book: On April 20, 1999, Hitler's birthday, uncontrolled anger, brought about by a lack of true values and principles, struck again. On that terrible day, in a typical urban setting, there were twelve students and one faculty member killed, along with more than twenty students seriously injured at Columbine High School in Littleton, Colorado. All of this took place at the hands of two deranged male students packing enough artillery prepared to kill hundreds.

The world is in the midst of a reactive form of violence. Teenage boys, and deranged men, are taking the law into their own hands, becoming not only judge and jury, but also executioner of others and the establishment around them, self-perceived to be their enemies.

With Columbine, Eric Harris and Dylan Klebold were latchkey social outcasts that hated jocks. Columbine consequently became one of the biggest hate crimes in American history. Jocks may have been the primary targets. Unfortunately, other students who got in the way were victimized as well.

The lack of inbred integrity, coupled with the culture of modern teenage life, along with the violent, in-your-face brainwashing media, as well as the peer pressure that teens are excessively exposed to these days, are the primary ingredients of an explosive recipe for these senseless and violent acts.

The American Medical Association, along with the American Psychological Association, have come together to openly proclaim that all of the violent media to which kids are exposed, including violent music, is making kids insensitive to violence itself. I think it's having an effect on all people in general and not just kids.

Under the influence of violent media and aggressive peer pressures, while lacking the character to make *wise choices*, certain young males in their teens and early twenties, along with certain adults, are presenting a real problem to our society. Some boys and men have gained the ability to not only prejudicially hate, but also lose all self-control and sensitivity, choosing to violently harm and/or kill others.

There was a day when young men were too busy, tending livestock and cultivating crops, to even *think* about getting in serious trouble. And if they dared to do so, there was always the effective deterrent of dad and his belt behind the woodshed. Whippings, as they were sometimes called, may not have been humane but were nevertheless effective.

While working as a substitute teacher for an alternative high school comprised of different or at-risk teens, I overheard one boy talking to a group of his peers. The boy openly commented to them that for a living, he'd *like to get paid to kill people* and said it as though he meant it. I never reported it to school officials, but I did mention it to one of the other instructors who didn't seem to be concerned. He said that this particular boy was always spouting off that way and that he posed no real threat. I wondered. The boy's array of openly exposed macho-looking tattoos and mannerisms should have been a red-flag warning. I decided it best to mind my own business, hoping the other instructor was right and that the lad was just being cocky with his peers in order to gain some kind of psychological social status. Still, it didn't sit right with me.

In my opinion, these types of learned attitudes need to end. Too many young people of the world are being far too angry and aggressive. Outside of defensive military combat situations, which have been proven to be not mentally or physically healthy themselves, there needs to be less tolerance of these attitudes and actions throughout society.

Regarding contributing influences, graphic violence in the media should be a prime suspect. Why do kids need to view a lot of blood and gore in order to be entertained? For that matter, why does anyone?

In the animal kingdom, it's natural for males to fight each other for status and position, like bull elk and bucks during the autumn rut. People, on the other hand, supposedly above animals, while perhaps having the desire to strangle each other at times, also have the freedom of choice to abstain from violence. Human beings, as the most intelligent species on Earth, though sometimes debatable, have the ability to use communication and negotiation to confront and solve our differences, rather than the use of physical violence. We shouldn't require horns, claws, or sharp teeth to deal with our perceived enemies. Neither should we require guns, knives, or bombs to solve our problems.

There have been a series of mass shootings around the world, some larger than others, all of them terrible tragedies. With Columbine, the perpetrators, Eric Harris, age 18, and Dylan Klebold, age 17, both wearing black trench coats, had plotted for a year to kill at least 500, and to blow up their school with explosives. Both committed suicide at the scene.

Though Columbine may have been one of the deadliest mass shootings on record, many others around the world have been worse.

Political leaders have gone so far as to blame the perpetrators of these mass killings, calling them *cowards*. They're not cowards. They're sick, deranged, immoral people with serious mental disturbances brought on by a sick, deranged, immoral society. So, we really have no one to blame but ourselves.

Outside of wars, which have killed millions, there have been thousands of people killed or injured in these incidents around the world. Fortunately, a number of other planned massacres have been foiled by increased law enforcement intelligence and no-tolerance efforts, as well as informed leads and tips. For example, not long after the Columbine shooting incident, there was a nineteen-year-old student from De Anza College in Cupertino, California, arrested for plotting to blow up and gun down crowds of students at his own college. He was apparently greatly influenced by the Columbine massacre, since his personal website proclaimed, *"Eric Harris is God."* Fortunately, an alert photo clerk developed some pictures of the boy brandishing pipe bombs and an arsenal of weapons and called the police.

As a teacher, I personally observed several kids still wearing black trench coats around the high school where I was teaching, less than two years after the Columbine incident. Additionally, there was a note left in the bathroom of another local high school threatening an event *bigger than Columbine.*

Since we, as a society, really haven't solved the root problems that lead to terrorism and violence, the senseless killing will continue.

As I indicated in the introduction, the situation in Littleton hit close to home for me, happening in the same school district where I attended. Furthermore, my sister and her family were living in Littleton at the time of the shooting. After Columbine, I became an advocate of responsible gun control, whereas prior to that, being a lifelong outdoorsman and hunter, I was totally on the side of the Second Amendment, along with the National Rifle Association (NRA). I had always felt, and still do, that it was the people *behind* the guns that committed murders, not the guns themselves. On the other hand, it's quite obvious to me now that when weapons (especially assault weapons) make it into the hands of deranged people, something drastic has to change. I'm still in favor of legal firearms, provided they remain secured in responsible hands. As long as we can maintain a moral society, our Constitution, as well as the *right to bear arms,* should remain safe and sound. The key word to consider here is *moral.* In a nonmoral society, weapons are not the root problem; lack of values and principles, normally instilled by quality principle-centered upbringings and family life, is the primary problem.

Responsibilities that are born and bred on these ideals are sorely missing from many segments of our society today, especially with so many abused, abandoned, neglected, and outcast children in the world. Additionally, kids coming from affluent families are not immune. Eric Harris and Dylan Klebold weren't exactly poverty cases.

I can understand the current frustrations that some of these kids are feeling; however, that doesn't give them the right to take out their frustrations with violence. Doing so is completely irresponsible, as much as throwing in the towel and committing suicide. But let's not just sit back and call them cowards. Instead, we should continue to identify those at risk and get them intensive professional help.

Much of it has to do with one's instilled ability to cope with one's surroundings. When I was in high school, I, too, couldn't stand egotistical jocks, preppies, bullies, etc., but I learned to live with them based on my own inbred values that my mother and grandmother taught me.

When it comes to coping (a form of self-discipline), if you never learned it at home, your ability to control yourself in all situations is at risk. Consequently, not being able to control the actions of others, one is more likely to harm in anger, especially if under the influence of alcohol and drugs. People who have been taught self-discipline have learned to control their emotions when things don't always go their way.

There *is* no excuse for killing another human being, under *any* circumstances, no matter *how* frustrated, angry, or depressed you become. Additionally, one needs to clean up one's act, take responsibility for one's own actions, and avoid violence and getting into trouble.

Many kids, not having father figures there for them while growing up, in addition to non-sports-minded mothers, are faced with a lack of coaching or pride and desire for them to excel in sports. Additionally, high school sports have historically, as well as recently, been so competitive that unless kids are in the caliber of athletic high performers, they'll often end up cut from the team, or *sitting the bench* as it's called. Due to financial situations, as well as social and political pressures within the schools, the coaches consequently have to seek out the jocks that excel. Back when I was going to school, many of the high school coaches, due to the politics of school sports, were unable to pay much attention to troubled and emotionally disturbed youth that may have just needed a little extra understanding, special coaching, or added encouragement. Outside of Special Olympics, things really haven't changed much. If you're an emotionally disturbed, troubled kid, who hasn't had much exposure to sports, getting cut from the team doesn't do much for your confidence and self-esteem. In those situations, society sends out a very strong message to its already at-risk kids, telling them they aren't good enough and to go away.

Mean jocks don't help matters much. In my opinion, there's always been an obvious distinction between respectable athletes, like Michael Jordan, and cocky jerks.

Recalling my high school years, it didn't take a genius to see what was going on in the social structure of our school. Golden High School, back in the late 1960s, wasn't much different than Columbine High School thirty years later. The only real difference was that some of the outcasts of the 1990s traded their switchblades for guns. Instead of being called *hoods*, they were calling themselves *Trench Coat Mafia*. Black leather jackets used to be adequate for hiding a switchblade, but now it took full trench coats to hide an assault rifle or a sawed-off shotgun. Other than that, there really isn't much difference between the teenage social structures of the 1960s, and those of the 1990s, except that the stakes got much higher as ethical standards declined.

Alcohol and substance abuse has always

been a problem, but it seems to be much worse now, due to the obvious and increasing breakdown of the family and the decline of morals in our society. Moreover, adults often are not the best role models. Additionally, our government isn't helping much while being lobbied by certain vice industries. Of all the resources going toward dealing with the effects of alcohol and substance abuse in America, how much is actually aimed at preventive measures. As with our system of justice, things are more reactive rather than proactive.

Alcohol, tobacco, and drugs in the United States is a multi-hundred-billion-dollar industry, with teenagers being major consumers of these products. Moreover, one out of four of all deaths in America are directly attributable to substance abuse.

Our public schools try to take on the responsibility of policing such problems, but this mostly has to be a function of quality upbringings and not the responsibility of the schools. Obviously, law enforcement has to enter the picture with the parents, if underage drinking is occurring in public places, but schools should be staying out of the parenting and policing business. The schools have a role in *educating* kids on the adverse effects and the risks of alcohol and substance abuse, as well as assisting parents in the teaching of ethics, but that role ends there. Underage drinking and substance abuse is nothing new in the world, but it is becoming more of a widespread problem as our society continues to lower its moral standards. Although short of ideal, I believe these standards were a notch higher in the past.

Obviously, there are a growing number of behavioral problems that revolve around troubled teens. With kids literally dying from violence in the streets and in our public schools, the time has come to face up to, properly manage, and tackle the root problems. Zero tolerance for violence in and around schools, as well as our neighborhoods, is a good place to start. However, we need to go a leap further and effectively go after the root causes of abuse, abandonment, neglect, and domestic violence in families. Sound principles need to be well established through childrearing, as well as formal education. Strict punishment for abuse and violence, or separating kids from their parents is not the complete answer. Awareness education for both kids *and* their parents is the best solution. You have to have a certain amount of education and experience to get a license to drive or fly; you should have to go through the same process, if not more so, to have children. Intelligence and awareness are the only things that will ever outweigh social ignorance.

Society needs to learn self-discipline in order to make *wise choices*. Many kids today are becoming problematic. For example, while I was teaching at a local middle school, the administrators discovered a knife on a boy that I had sent to the office for gross misbehavior. Because of a no-tolerance policy for violence and weapons, the police were brought in and hauled the boy off to the police station. I imagine his parent(s), after receiving the phone call at work or home, may have been shocked over the whole matter, or perhaps not – a lot of dysfunctional kids may have dysfunctional parents.

Another related situation that happened at that same school involved a drunken mother slamming into another car while on school premises during school hours. The poor little girl, belonging to this intoxicated parent, stood by and watched while the police hauled her mother off to jail in front of God and everyone. Incidentally, that same girl was enrolled in special education classes for emotionally disturbed children. Is it any wonder?

Finally, at this same average American school, on the one-year anniversary of the Columbine tragedy, the police had to arrest another young boy, after he had made threatening remarks to some of the other students. These kids had gone home and told their parents about it, and consequently, there were a lot of children that didn't show up for school that next day which has also happened during Columbine anniversaries at many other schools.

Most of these occurrences don't usually make it to the local news, let alone national and international news, unless there's loss of lives involved. It makes you wonder just how many of these disturbing situations are happening around the world. Fortunately, most continue to be detected and stopped before they go too far.

Family domestic situations are usually the cause of disfunction in troubled teens. The effects of these problems come in many forms and have many disguises. Symptoms can surface in the form of moodiness, depression, anger, physical anomalies, and phobias, as well as a whole spectrum of other psychological disorders. Domestic violence and abuse, along with neglect, are common causes in the emergence of troubled teens. From a management perspective, as with any problem or illness, most professionals will admit that *prevention* is the best medicine. We need to get away from the mindset of after-the-fact reactive correction and punitive measures as control mechanisms and into the mindset of prevention and/or rehabilitation. That takes getting to the source of these situations before children become too deeply disturbed.

Furthermore, dysfunction has no real preference as to economic class or social structure. It doesn't root itself strictly among the poor, even though prison and jail populations would tend to not support that reasoning with the majority of prisoners being from nonaffluent families. In many instances, provided you can afford the right attorneys, you can actually buy yourself out of trouble. After all, if the glove does not fit, you must acquit, right? There's a long list of dysfunctional problems that have surfaced throughout affluent and famous families around the world. These people don't seem to spend much time, if any, in jail, and when they do, they usually aren't there very long. When it comes to rich kids, they may have plenty of money but are often starved of time, attention, and love from their parents. Even though the masses of poor outnumber the rich; proportionately, there are just as many dysfunctional families among the rich and famous as there are among the impoverished villages, trailer parks, and slums across the country. It's just that one side has *too* much money for their own good, and the other side doesn't have enough. Both extremes can lead to criminal behavior, be it blue collar *or* white collar. The middle class, although not without their share of problems, are relatively stable, compared to the other two extremes.

There are a lot of good kids out there. However, there is a growing number of kids that, due to their personal life situations and negative or skewed perceptions of the world around them, do not adjust nearly as well. These are the kids that display emotionally disturbed behaviors and who can present taxing problems, especially for substitute teachers. Grades seven through nine are unquestionably the most challenging. That's the age group where unprincipled games and trickery such as *Sink the Sub* are most prevalent.

I found that *management style* and the principles of *situational leadership* are critical tools while dealing with teens. Some need highly autocratic and authoritative management, and the ones that don't still need support and encouragement. It really depends on the young individual and his or her personal situation; sometimes it just depends on the day.

I had my share of subbing physical education classes, and one that I liked the most was high school walking class. A lot of people may ask why schools need to teach teenagers how to walk.

For everyone, walking is probably one of the best forms of physical and cardiovascular exercise. Additionally, long walks can also be mentally therapeutic. As for teenagers, with all of the commercial junk food they consume, and the social stress they experience, they need to get in the habit of exercising it off. Also, walking makes one gain an appreciation for his or her natural surroundings, as opposed to being glued to electronic devices.

I don't know about other PE teachers, but I personally used walking classes to metaphorically demonstrate to the students the importance of pacing yourself to keep up with the rest of the group – keeping up with society, if you will.

Before we left the building, I would spell out the *rules of the road, or path* to them:

(Rule A) They needed to stay together as a group. That meant no one was to go ahead, take off on his or her own agenda, or lag behind in a leisurely stroll.

(Rule B) I would set the pace for the group. If they couldn't keep up with me, a person they probably considered an old man, then they had a real problem with their personal level of physical fitness.

(Rule C) Somewhere along the way, at my discretion, I would stop and take attendance. Anyone not present would be marked absent, which always resulted in a call to his or her parents by the school administration later that day. Anyone lagging way behind would be counted as tardy, which usually resulted in a discounted grade in that class for the day.

With these rules in mind, I explained to them that the walk was not only a physical exercise but was also a mental exercise, according to the rules, and to think about the reasons *why* in the course of the walk. That brought not only a lot of crazy comments but also a number of puzzled looks, as though they were thinking, *who is this guy, anyway?*

At the end of the class, when we all got back to the building, I would ask the group to explain to me both the physical as well as the mental benefits of what we just did. Being a PE class, most of them were able to give me fairly good answers as to the *physical* benefits. Some of them grasped the mental reasoning behind it, but most just didn't get it. For those who didn't, whether they actually cared or not, I then proceeded to explain the metaphorical reasoning of the exercise to them.

(Reason A) As they walk through the rest of their lives, they have a *choice*. They can either independently ignore what society is dishing out – taking off on their own agendas (society dropouts) or not keep up (lagging behind in a leisurely stroll through life). Or, they can stick with and contribute to the mainstream of society.

(Reason B) Those in political power and control will always set the pace for the rest of society – get used to it. If you want to change the rules of the road, then gain legitimate political power and control to do so (i.e., become a teacher or a politician).

(Reason C) Somewhere along the way, those who are in power and control are going to be holding you accountable. If you're not conforming to the rules of society and the laws of government, you will be subjected to the politics and punishment that society dishes out to those who don't conform.

I always advise young people to get used to the politics of power and control, because that part of society will not likely change in the foreseeable future. As for power, it comes in many forms. There is the power of love and respect (caring), which is associated with a modern form of management called *leadership*. There is the power of fear and intimidation, associated with autocratic control (old-school, traditional management). There is power in having information and knowledge that others do not have. Lastly, there is materialistic power in possessing physical resources (to include money) that others do not possess. Not all of them being concepts found at the forefront of teenage motivation.

In any case, there will always be those who possess more of these powers than others. However, *knowledge* is the one form of power that, once you have grasped it, no one can take it from you. In that respect, we should study and learn as much as we can throughout our entire lives. Many have claimed, and I would highly agree, *Knowledge is power*. In today's litigious and competitive world, unless you're smarter than the next guy, you can get beat up just as bad *mentally* as you can *physically*.

As far as those school walking classes went, I don't think the symbolism meant much to most of those teenagers. However, I do hope a few of them paid attention and will remember those walks, integrating them into future behavior.

I love playing with kids' heads in a positive and productive way. For me, that has always been one of the greatest rewards of teaching in or out of school. I can only hope that I made a few young people stop and think, even if they didn't quite get it at the time.

By the tenth grade, most young people start to reach a higher level of maturity, and by the time they become juniors and seniors in high school, the majority of them really start to pull things together (as much as teenagers can) as they approach early adulthood.

When these young people walk out of their high schools for the last time, as they head for college, trade school, the military, or wherever life takes them, they soon find themselves at that magic age of eighteen and suddenly legal adults. Most of them quickly learn that they are now more susceptible as well as liable to the punitive, litigious, and social states of our society. Knowing that, many come to realize that should they happen to make a serious social or legal mistake, it could unfortunately impact them for the rest of their lives. Sadly, some *never* learn.

Persistent Prematurity

Carry on Wayward Son
— Kansas

It's oddly predictable how so many people suddenly, at the stroke of midnight, on their eighteenth birthday, leave their premature teenage years behind to become election-voting, war-fighting, cigarette-smoking, lottery-playing, legal adults. Well, almost adults anyway.

At no point in the course of our lives is the need and ability to make *wise choices* greater than between the ages of eighteen and twenty-one. At that juncture, people will either choose *positive* roads to take or *negative* ones. If they're smart, possess good character traits and have enough self-discipline, they'll choose positive paths. It's that simple, but due to all of the vast and growing temptations available in our free society, young adults often become sidetracked. Consequently, the age of eighteen becomes a crucial turning point of managing life.

I finally figured out something at the age of seventeen going on eighteen, as I was graduating from high school during the height of the Vietnam War, with the military draft system breathing down my neck. I got to thinking that if it weren't for the need for eighteen to twenty-one-year-olds in the military, the legal age for *all* vices would have probably been steadfastly set at the age of twenty-one where it really *should* be. However, since we're asking these less-than-mature adults to go help fight our wars for us, then I suppose we had better be prepared to give them the legal right to partake in the same vices readily indulged in by *mature* adults. It's only fair, as long as we're asking them to risk their lives for their country.

Ironically, the American society still refuses to allow eighteen to twenty-one-year-olds to drink alcoholic beverages. We eighteen-year-olds, back in my time, used to be allowed to drink 3.2 beer that we called *near-beer*, but civilization has since taken that privilege away. In grown-up America's eyes, eighteen to twenty-one-year-olds are still premature adults and are not quite ready for old John Barleycorn. Furthermore, they're just not quite *mature* enough to be sitting around, pulling slot machine handles, or to be betting on sports, but since state lotteries support civic causes, it's okay for them to partake in these forms of so-called *good* gambling. Additionally, it's also okay, in the name of democracy and freedom, to slap an assault weapon into eighteen-year-old hands and require them, under military law and strict orders, to kill other human beings different from us, but it's a capital crime to kill each other. No wonder young people become so confused.

It's bizarre how our society has made it legal for the military to kill foreigners presumed to be our enemies, but should we become a threat to fellow countrymen – well, that's against the law. From a national perspective, I can understand this situation, but from a global or universal perspective, it seems somewhat of a special interest or double standard.

Meanwhile people throughout the world continue lying, cheating, stealing, and killing one another – justified in their own minds. These things happen every day and have become commonplace in some unethical cultures. The news we see, read, and hear each and every day continues to remind us of the reality of it all, no matter how much we try to ignore it.

As I started writing this book right after the Columbine tragedy, I suddenly realized that something was drastically going wrong in the world. Since then, these problems have clearly surfaced in the minds of many of us. To support what I'm talking about, hear the words of a father whose daughter, at Columbine, was suddenly killed at the hands of two crazed boys simply because she openly proclaimed her faith in God.

Darrell Scott (in part) before Congress:

"Since the dawn of creation, there has been both good and evil in the hearts of men and women. We all contain the seeds of kindness or the seeds of violence. The death of my wonderful daughter, Rachel Joy Scott, and the deaths of that heroic teacher and the other eleven children who

died must not be in vain. Columbine was not just a tragedy; it was a spiritual event that should be forcing us to look at where the real blame lies! I wrote a poem that expresses my feelings best":

Your laws ignore our deepest needs; your words are empty air. You've stripped away our heritage; you've outlawed simple prayer. Now gunshots fill our classrooms, and precious children die. You seek for answers everywhere, and ask the question "Why?" You regulate restrictive laws, through legislative creed. And yet you fail to understand that God is what we need!

Scott went on to say, "*Men and women are three-part beings. We all consist of body, soul, and spirit. When we refuse to acknowledge a third part of our makeup, we create a void that allows evil, prejudice, and hatred to rush in and wreak havoc. What has happened to us as a nation? We have refused to honor God, and in so doing, we open the doors to hatred and violence. We need a change of heart and humble acknowledgment that this nation was founded on the principle of simple trust in God!*"

Many, including Congress, may take offense at Darrell Scott's words, yet America continues to falter from its original charter (the Constitution) where spiritual faith in God, outside of any single religion, was, at one time, a right not challenged. Congress, for the most part, is no longer making unbiased decisions based on *ethical principle*;

rather, it too often is making *lobbied* choices based on material gains. In fact, to our disbelief, it has now become almost an under-the-table requirement within these circles if one wants to keep his or her political career intact.

All I can say is, God help the world and save it from greed and corruption! Perhaps it would help us to look at the entire situation from a different perspective. Pretend you're a highly intelligent being from another part of the universe remotely observing Earth's human behaviors, or shall we say, *misbehaviors*. You possess a technology that makes jet aircraft look like ancient, primitive artifacts. You no longer have a single, perceived enemy in the entire universe. You have since traded your scarcity mentality and prejudice for greater knowledge, wisdom, and understanding. Your source of energy is light-years beyond fossil fuels, and the mental gap between you and the beings you are observing is so vast that effective communication would be virtually impossible. You have the undeniable ability to solve every single one of their problems, yet that would be a futile effort due to the primitive, competitive nature and culture of these creatures. Most of them just wouldn't get it, no matter how well you explained or presented it to them. Their only hope is to naturally evolve together to reach and discover higher knowledge and wisdom for themselves, provided they can do that before they reach a point of self-destruction and extinction. One of the biggest threats to we humans is the environmental threat of global warming and climate change. RIBBIT

So, is it possible for us primitive beings to begin to wise up and change in order to fend off our biggest threats? I think so, provided we put enough intelligence, wisdom, and scientific technology to work.

Other than climate change, another one of our biggest threats is for the world to continue senseless wars. At some point, we have to lay down the weapons and stop killing each other, especially considering the number of nuclear arsenals around the world. With killing, justified or not, I think the point to be made is that *all* human life is precious. No populace should be the selective victims of any other populace's prejudice. Unfortunately, with the current unenlightened population, self-perceived enemies seem to be fair game. In the case of *foreign* enemies, perhaps war and killing is unavoidable when certain countries are forced to take defensive action against offensive and evil aggressors. Hitler would be a classic example of this type of barbarian. Unethical aggressors and fascists dictators all come from the same mold. As an example, interestingly, with Saddam Hussein who was an authoritarian dictator of Iraq between 1979 and 2003, we have someone who was raised without a natural father and who was seriously abused by his stepfather. That brings us back to the theory of parenting as a possible root problem.

Furthermore, Saddam's late sons were also raised to be much like him. Unfortunately for the world, irresponsible parenting has a very bad habit of reproducing and perpetuating irresponsible offspring. What a shame it is that so many people have had to suffer at the hands of inhumane and prejudiced dictators throughout history. If these tyrants were raised with principle-centered ethics, these sorts of catastrophes would come to an end and would cease to exist in the future. I cautiously have faith that unenlightened people become enlightened and will eventually transform humanity in the right direction.

We should ask ourselves, why has all this violence been going on throughout history and why is it that people continue to hate each other so much? Could it be greed and jealousy that are causing the resulting prejudice, brought about by a lack of instilled moral code? Could it have something to do with the scarcity of ethics, integrity, and character in our world society? When will we come to our senses and finally learn that war and fighting *have never* and *will never* solve our problems? It will only act to stir the hornet's nest and feed upon its own negative existence. When will we come to our senses and realize that the true problem is the lack of genuine, unselfish, unconditional love and respect for each other? And when will we come to our senses to realize that no nation is completely innocent and without its share of guilt? When and if we, as a world society, finally take the responsibility to positively solve the roots of our worst problems, then, and only then can there be lasting world peace.

A point to be made and reiterated in this chapter is that premature adults are being taught the wrong things while treated as, and given the privileges and vices of adults, before they are either physically or emotionally capable of taking on that level of responsibility. Realistically, eighteen-year-olds are not and will never be considered actual grownups by the rest of the so-called grown-up population but are necessarily allowed, as well as required, to take on that role when domestic and world situations dictate.

In relation to this unwise situation, I would like to insert a column written by a young lady editor of a local high school newspaper where I was once teaching. She had just turned eighteen. In her column, she wrote:

I feel like so many different messages are being sent my way concerning adulthood.

By turning eighteen, I am now allowed to do so many things that I wasn't legally allowed to do before. For instance, I can now buy myself cigarettes, tobacco products and pornography, although I am interested in none of the above. I can buy myself lottery tickets and I can vote in national and local elections. If I were a boy, I could be sent off to war.

My parents also have the right to kick me out of the house if they feel it is needed.

Now, any illegal acts that I am caught doing will be placed on my permanent criminal record and I will be tried as an adult. That's right, as an ADULT. I am legally considered an adult but the attendance office still calls my parents if I ditch a class!

I feel no different than I did when I was seventeen, except now I know that I am considered more responsible and trustworthy of my own decisions.

It seems strange that in one day they, the nebulous they, think that I am responsible enough to do all of these things that I couldn't do the day before.

I don't quite understand the mixed emotions that our society and country send us about becoming adults. They tell me that I am now grown-up enough to be sent off to war and die, but I am not responsible enough to drink alcohol. Along with gambling, that is the one thing that I can think of that I am unable to do. It really makes no sense and using logic makes it more confusing.

Think about It: I can die in war, but I cannot drink alcohol. I can die with a cigarette in my mouth, but I cannot drink alcohol. It seems so contradictory.

Why is it that when you turn twenty-one you are allowed to drink? 21-year-olds seem no more mature when it comes to responsible drinking than do eighteen-year-olds.

To me, it seems as though I am being used. If our country needs an eighteen-year-old to die for them, they have every right to use us. To fulfill its needs, it uses us. But on the flip side, if we want to drink, we can't. It's a mixed signal. And morally, I really don't think it's right or justified.

I would much rather have one set age that we are considered adults, it would make more sense and life would be a heck of a lot easier.

Either tell us we're adults at eighteen or at twenty-one, but give us all of the privileges at once rather than over time.

So, there you have it, straight from the mouth of babes. But then, what does she know? She's just a kid…not even twenty-one yet!

Seriously, I must say that I completely agree with this young lady.

Objectively, no one, especially premature teenage adults, should *ever* be sent off under *any* circumstances to die fighting *any* war. However, in this still primitive world we live in, we simply would not have the number of troops required and available to maintain a superior international status and strength without eighteen to twenty-one-year-olds serving in the armed forces. That's the real issue after all, is it not? We, the over-twenty-one-year-old adults, would never actually consider anyone under the age of twenty-one a full adult, would we? It's just that we have been required by global situations to conveniently delegate at least a portion of our dirty work to the eighteen to twenty-one-year-olds in order to sustain a free and democratic society. What a shame it is that we, along with the rest of the world, have been politically and punitively forced by each other to have to do these things for our own perceived, justifiable good. When it comes to national defense, it's a crying shame that we humans have to protect ourselves from each other. When and where, not to mention how, will this vicious and violent circle ever be broken?

We already have so very much experience of too many destructive, unproductive wars. Clearly, the ability to end this dilemma rests with continually increasing the average level of intelligence in the world. Knowledge is the road that leads to the wisdom of love and respect for other human beings. Therefore, knowledge is not only *power,* it is also the seed of *peace.*

Even though evidence of growing ignorance abounds with some of the idiotic things some people seem to continually do, there is solid evidence that the majority of our society, as a whole, is actually becoming more intelligent. According to *U.S. News & World Report,* at the end of the last decade, Americans, making up less than 5 percent of the world's population, won 56 percent of the Nobel Prizes in economics, 45 percent in physics, and 57 percent in medicine.

Additionally, national tests showed improvement in reading and math among elementary students, and there were more people attending colleges and universities than ever before. More impressively, the average IQ score in America rose fifteen points since the 1940s. That said, provided the rest of the world follows, lasting world peace may actually be possible, that is if education doesn't deteriorate in the meantime. Other than the deviation of education, unscrupulous characteristics such as jealousy, inflated egos, anger, greed, and corruption will only act to ultimately keep the human race from crossing the finish line of world peace as well.

Islam philosophy states, *"The ink of a scholar is far more precious than the blood of a martyr."* Radical Islamic terrorists should heed their own philosophy. If one does not like the way the world is going, then one should obtain enough knowledge and have enough character to take out a *pen* rather than a weapon. As it's also been said, the pen is, in fact, mightier than the sword. I would add that it is the mind, through knowledge, that powers the pen. Further, all the bullets, explosives, and weapons of mass destruction in the world don't hold a candle to the combined power of enlightened human minds.

Theoretically, I believe that someday, the world *can* reach that enduring and dynamic level of intelligence required for everlasting world peace, whereby communication and negotiation will take the place of wars and the extermination of one another. Unfortunately for the world, I don't think any of this will take place any time soon. More than likely, it will take at least another generation or so, but I hope and pray we people don't wait too much longer, since time is quickly running out. Perhaps the current increasingly knowledgeable young people of the world are the long-awaited keys to a peaceful future. Previous generations have all had their opportunities but have obviously failed miserably.

With my generation, the post-World War II baby boomers, we may have greatly contributed to many of the milestones in technology and better living through the arts and sciences, but many of us have forgotten ethics and values and have become far too materialistic for our own foreseeable good. Much of that may have to do with the way we were raised by our parents, who wanted to give us everything they perceivably never had.

Growing up in sheltered environments, few of us had to personally deal with major world crises. I can distinctly remember entering adulthood, back when America was, for the most part, a safe and secure nation. Sure, the Vietnam war was still going on, but for those of us who were not directly involved, that was just something remotely happening on the other side of the world. Today, with modern technology, transportation, and communications, the Middle

East, as well as the Far East, are now as close as our televisions. With Earth becoming a virtually smaller, more populated place, world unrest and violence have reached a new dimension, and whether we like it or not, it's now in our own living rooms. As the world's population continues to grow out of control, without enough knowledge and wisdom to go along, so do its associated problems.

In the last half of the twentieth century, many premature adults, including myself, began to take freedom, democracy, and personal possessions too much for granted. Many of us, leaving home and going off to college, either forgot or didn't bother to pack important values, principles, and self-discipline in with our stereo equipment. Previous generations – our parents and grandparents, experiencing economically devastating events like the Depression, World War II, and more challenging lifestyles due to the lack of money and modern technology – experienced tougher times.

Leaving home at the age of seventeen without money or materialistic crutches, I suppose I had an advantage in having enough room in my suitcase to pack a few instilled character traits. One disadvantage that I would run into, however, would be the powerful peer pressure from a modern young society.

It was a strange and unnerving experience to go off to college. Considering my options, I had the choices of an all-expense-paid trip to the tropical rain forests of Vietnam, enter the Air Force Academy, or I could opt to go to a state college with a college deferment. Besides, I had a high lottery number at the time as well. Under the circumstances, given the choices, it was a no-brainer. I saw what war does to people, including what it had done to my own father, so I decided on education instead. Even though I felt bad for all the soldiers that did end up in Vietnam, some of them my own friends, I couldn't allow myself to feel guilty for not going myself. However, my hat is respectfully off to all of the veterans who've served in both foreign and domestic wars. We should never take what they fought for, freedom and democracy, for granted.

As a premature adult, away from home, I was suddenly at a point in my life where I was completely on my own, with no immediate family available to confide in or give me refuge when I needed it.

Upon arriving at college, I immediately was taken in by the array of loud music coming from the open dorm windows. In the late summer of 1970, Vietnam-related tunes, along with the original Woodstock music, amplified with giant stereo systems, were the most popular among college kids. Some of these huge stereos, which could have easily served as public address systems in sports arenas, were typically set up in cozy ten-by-twenty-foot dorm rooms. The music was so loud, I could distinctly hear it from where I was in the parking lot.

In any event, there I was, having to do some serious adjusting to a new lifestyle. In my new home away from broken home, it was time for me to either sink or swim. I recalled a time when the lifeguard had to fish me out of the pool with a long pole while taking swimming lessons at the YMCA. Keeping one's head above water can be a real challenge whether you're in a swimming pool or a social pool. In either case, if you don't have the right instruction and skills, you're sunk.

A principle of managing life: *Adult guidance and mentoring, when available, can become a vital asset during trying and/or traumatic life transitions.*

Considering peer pressure and making *wise choices,* in the autumn of 1970, my hair looked like I had just stepped out of a redneck barbershop. In these new surroundings, that would soon change. The guys from places like Chicago and Los Angeles, with the killer stereos and all the girls hanging around them, had shoulder-length hair and radical T-shirts and wore weird-smelling aftershave. They also were smoking funny cigarettes. I, no doubt, had some catching up to do if I wanted to fit in and actually swim with these guys.

That year, it didn't take me long to alter my taste in music, grow my hair out, and change my style a bit. I personally didn't drink alcohol or do drugs back in high school, as some did, but was now socially pressured to either adopt certain vices and attitudes or sit the bench with the rest of the perceived studious geeks and nerds. Without needed guidance at that point in my life, I allowed the peer pressure to take over. Unfortunately, there was a time when it became more powerful than my ability to make *wise choices*.

I started hanging out at parties and frequenting the local near-beer joints with my buddies, and giving in to certain temptations. At the time, we didn't see ourselves as being unprincipled. In our minds, it was just a normal part of being in college.

Things obviously haven't changed much over the years with so many alcohol and drug related injuries and deaths at the college-age level in the United States each year. No matter what the law dictates for age requirements, college kids will always be able to get their hands on all the vices they choose. We should go back in history and study *Prohibition* to really understand how ineffective laws can be when it comes to controlling alcohol consumption. The same goes for drugs, gambling, pornography, and other bad habits. Obviously, the war on drugs has been failing for a long time due to obsessive demand that illegal supply will always meet. Realistically, the only things that can actually control vices are strong principle-centered values and enough self-discipline to abstain. A simple principle of business management is that the supply will dry up if the demand for products and services goes away. In that respect, with substance abuse, the wisdom to *just say no* curbs demand.

We each have power within us to control temptations, passions, and desires that weigh us down and keep us from obtaining what we truly want out of life but fail to understand. The deal is, how much do we truly desire to make *wise choices* in order to reach our goals? Do we even have goals? Without them, it's true, *we will continue to aim at nothing and succeed.*

With all the partying, I really don't know how I succeeded at getting the passing grades I did those first couple of years at college. Maybe, in addition to acting stupid, I was just naturally smart. Some kids aren't so fortunate and end up flunking out. You know what they say about all work and no play. Well, all play and no work doesn't cut it either. Once again, it all comes down to instilled self-discipline and making good *choices*. Self-discipline is one of the most important character traits people can give their children; a trait they will use to succeed all their lives, especially when they leave home and are forced to fend for themselves in the world.

As a universal principle, every challenging situation comes down to making *wise choices*.

Another universal principle of life to consider: *Misguided planning leads to poor management*. Throughout their late teens and early twenties, I think a lot of misguided kids, leaving home and finding themselves alone in this scary, crazy world, having to make it on their own, have the potential risk of developing some bad habits and vices, potentially leading to lifelong personal problems. I would again importantly reiterate that nowhere in the course of their lives, due to the peer pressures and cultures that exist around them, are young people ever more challenged to make proper choices. Instilled values and principles, as well as family guidance, surely become a critical defense mechanism at that maturing stage.

It seems that many young adults these days are attracted to glamorous places like Hollywood, New York City, and Washington, D.C., determined to make it big, reaching out for fame and fortune. Hollywood is best known for its entertainment celebrity. New York City is known for big businesses, as well as entertainment. But Washington always has been, is, and always will be the hub of America.

Considering the world of politics, there are young people that enter that arena with the best intentions of nobly changing the world for the better. Unfortunately, they soon run into the *politics of politics*. Some survive, most, however, fail to make the grade. Usually, the ones who succeed do so through influence, connections, and political contacts. Like chess, it often becomes a game of strategy or kings of the mountain, so to speak. In America's case, the mountain happens to be Capitol Hill.

Additionally, Capitol Hill will weave its golden, political threads back and forth with big business and Hollywood alike and will in turn have *its* back scratched. The official term, considering these politics, is called *lobbying*. All become associated and affiliated through common values (fame, fortune, status, and ego). Inappropriately, for the common people of the world, global markets and the economy are driven by these influential, materialistic, and non-principled values.

Let's look at some of the ethical standards exhibited on Capitol Hill at the turn of this last century. Of the 535 members of the United States Congress:

- 29 were accused of spousal abuse.
- 7 were arrested for fraud.
- 19 were accused of writing bad checks.
- 117 directly or indirectly bankrupted at least two businesses.
- 3 served time for assault.
- 71 couldn't get a credit card due to bad credit.
- 14 were arrested on drug-related charges.
- 8 were arrested for shoplifting.
- 21 were defendants in lawsuits.
- 84 were arrested for drunk driving.

We won't get into the world of entertainment, but it's safe to assume that these types of behaviors existed at the same time in Hollywood. Things don't seem to have improved much since.

Will there ever be ethical behavior and justice? Let's not be fooled. White-collar arrests are rarely anything more than public pacifiers. Expecting Capitol Hill to clean up the corporate world is like asking the fox to clean up the hen house. One way or another, America needs to clean up Capitol Hill first and foremost before it ever stands a chance of cleaning up the rest of the country. Our deepest problems need to be solved from the top-down while being controlled from the bottom up.

Be it business and political gangs or street gangs, sturdy values and principles are too often missing today.

Frequently, young adults, mostly males that hang out within groups or gangs, can get into a lot of trouble. Similar to Capitol Hill, in the case of street gangs, the initiation processes and the peer pressures involved dictate the actions of the entire group. Furthermore, in these situations, members, especially new members, dare not show any reluctance or fear, or their peers will reject and label them. Or worse, they could be seriously injured or, God forbid, die at the hands of the other members that have established power within these gangs. It's gotten so bad in our inner cities that law enforcement can't effectively control it anymore. With hundreds of gang-related homicides per year, Police Departments have had their hands full, sometimes tied, trying to deal with it all.

Due to overpowering factors, it seems that making decisions at the crossroads of life often become a social choice rather than an individual choice. Due to the peer pressures involved, *wise choices* are often not made. With many boys, take a splash of testosterone, add a dash of adrenaline and an ounce or more of alcohol along with the drug of their choosing, mix them all up, and you've just created a recipe for trouble.

However, there *is* something along with education that can act to keep these young people out of trouble, and that is the action of burning off restless energy with healthy, legal, physical activities. Thus, we have the added value of recreation and disciplined sports for young people.

Coach John Wooden, whose leadership led UCLA to achieve some rather outstanding achievements in basketball, had a no-nonsense management style. A primary reason for UCLA's success on the court was that coach Wooden demanded an unprecedented level of self-discipline from each and every one of his players. He would instruct them, "*Discipline yourself so that others don't have to.*" Good advice for anyone.

It's funny how, presented with so many choices, a person's upbringing and life experiences can act to pull them, like a magnet, through the rest of their life. People sometimes use the excuse of being painted into corners (having no choice), but it often comes down to undisciplined personal decisions.

How can young people who are on the verge of becoming adult members of our society ever make *wise choices* in life without the guidance and direction of principle-centered influences and role models like coach Wooden? Once again, it all comes down to effective mentoring and early teaching of self-discipline.

After *premature adults* have reached the legal age of twenty-one, they are then considered by society to be more mature, *responsible adults* – at least by definition and expectation. Like many adults, however, due to less-than-responsible choices, a good number of them are still about a yard short of the goal of becoming completely responsible and dependable.

Responsible Adults

I'm Bad, I'm Nationwide

— ZZ Top

Terms that are self-contradictory or words that are incongruent with each other are referred to as *oxymorons*, such as, *responsible adults*. Many adults consider themselves to be responsible, but as imperfect human beings with biased perceptions and special interests, they might not be quite as responsible as they think or portray themselves to be.

Historically, we've all been fooling ourselves. The global adult population, in general, is anything *but* responsible. Just look around. Rarely in human history has there not been wars going on in the world. Additionally, crime and civil unrest abound everywhere. If societies were responsible, these things would not be going on to the degree that they are. People do have the ability to make *choices* but often fail to make them *wisely* in order to obtain a responsible and peaceful outcome.

As the human population further expands and concentrates itself in limited metropolitan areas, the more critical it will become for people to learn to get along with one another in a fair and equitable manner with complete trust. Otherwise, crime, unrest, territorial fighting and wars will only intensify and become even more prevalent in the future.

Sure, violence, and the fight or flight syndrome, may have been hardwired into our biology or neurological makeup since the cavemen, but that doesn't mean that an enlightened society can't learn to exchange *survival of the fittest* for *survival of the wisest*. I believe and have faith that we are now getting closer, with each passing millennium, to that very juncture, but humanity needs to seriously wise up before we destroy ourselves along with the rest of the planet.

We ought to wonder why places like Disneyland continue to be so successful. The likely answer is because *there*, in an effort to *get away from it all* in *fantasyland*, people can escape from the real world, at least temporarily. Unfortunately, we live in a place where people need to find fairytale escapes now and then, in order to maintain their sense of sanity. All of us, deep down, wish that life *was* a Disneyland, or a paradise found somewhere over the rainbow, but sadly, due to our misguided decisions and human imperfections, it's too often not that. Realistically, since we *can* envision it, that idealistic paradise over that rainbow could in fact exist, but only through *choices* based on wisdom can we ever possess and control the ability to reach out and achieve it. Instead of focusing on fictional ideals, we should be concentrating our attention, resources, and energy on seriously changing the world around us to *be* more idyllic rather than escaping harsh realities.

In the past, traditional families used to be supportive havens and escapes from the ugliness of the real world, but many families and homes have since become broken. Remember classic shows like *Lassie, The Waltons,* or *Little House on the Prairie*? Many adolescents in today's impersonal and insensitive world couldn't begin to identify with those shows. Even if they could, they'd probably be completely bored from the lack of action, sex, and violence.

I'm reminded of a time while working as an installation and service rep for a major aerial tramway manufacturer, I spent almost all of my time with fellow workers and virtually none of it with family. After many tedious, long hours, days, and months, one project after another, over the course of several years, I got tired of that routine and became dismayed. Lift installers' wives were referred to as lift widows. The few times I did get home to see my wife, I no longer recognized her. She had lost a great deal of weight and didn't appear very healthy or happy. With our having to be separated so much, our level of communication and relationship had begun to deteriorate. Unequivocally, I was starting to lose my health and happiness too.

Not long after that, I *chose* to leave that job.

Throughout my adult career, like many other people, I have constantly struggled with the meaning of what is responsible and what isn't. Is keeping a job and career that you value for materialistic and/or egotistic reasons worth it when it is destroying your family life? Often, too much time in the field or at the office leads to broken hearts and broken homes. Other times, the money being made may tend to compensate for the resulting neglect, but the situation can have a tendency to eat away at fragile relationships, much like flowing rivers and streams eventually act to erode mountains.

For a lot of overachievers, at the end of their careers, their families may *physically* still be there, but *mentally* and *spiritually*, they may have, in essence, separated themselves. This, in many cases, results in members of the family simply going their own way each day, hardly acknowledging one another. So, why do we allow this to happen? Earlier, we discussed the obsession of people to become rich or to climb higher on the ladder of success than the next guy. It's not called keeping up with the Joneses anymore. It has now evolved into passing the Joneses, selfishly racing ahead, always wanting more. Many people have become so materialistic that nothing else seems to matter. Just having a car isn't always good enough, it often has to be a status symbol. Just having a roof over our heads isn't enough either, it now has to be bigger and better than others' houses. Just having a job that pays the bills with a reasonable savings margin is no longer adequate; people have been known to claw their way up the competitive ladder, sometimes ruthlessly, in order to obtain more money and status over others.

I recall reading a newspaper article once that talked about the outlandish compensation rates of corporate executives, despite, in many cases, negative shareholder returns in their companies. In economic downturns, thousands of blue-collar workers can end up losing their jobs when CEOs who are making hundreds of times more than the workers stay employed, or, under contract, they end up with lucrative golden parachutes. It's strange how, even in softening economies, executives' pay continues to rise, and how CEOs have gotten rich, even when their companies don't always perform well. So, where's the accountability and responsibility, not to mention the business ethics in these companies and their executives? How can these businesses continue to function as healthy organizations?

Samuel Gompers originally formed trade unions in America due to gross inequalities in compensation, unfair working conditions imposed on labor, and other unethical business practices displayed by upper management. Gompers, a cigar maker by trade, was president of the American Federation of Labor for almost forty years, between 1886 and 1924, and the nation's leading trade unionist and labor spokesman. Thanks to him, unions started out with the best intentions of standing up for labor, but due to greed, other union organizers slowly became as corrupt as the companies they stood against.

If employers would remain responsible, equitable, and ethical in their business practices, from the top down, we wouldn't *have* the need for unions.

I haven't been able to justify any reasoning behind this sort of financial pomposity and arrogance displayed by the leadership of large corporations outside of the excuse used by irresponsible children – *Everyone else is doing it!* Meaning, CEOs are demanding and expecting giant compensation packages, only because others are getting them. It goes to show that some adults have a hard time growing up. They probably just weren't listening as children when their parents told them – *Just because everyone else is doing it doesn't mean it's right.* That is, provided their parents ever gave them that sound advice in the first place. Capitol Hill is just as guilty. As we've seen, politicians are well known to be lobbied and influenced by many of these major corporations.

Due to the greed factor, graduating from Harvard Business School today doesn't necessarily assure proper business ethics or responsible management. Greed is an extremely powerful force in the world that gets certain aggressive and competitive people exactly where *they* want to be at the expense, exploitation, and sometimes, devastation of others.

It was J. P. Morgan who suggested that a reasonable ratio of top management pay to that of the average worker should be twenty to one. Today, it's about three hundred to one. *No one* at the very top of *any* organization deserves to make that much, no matter *who* they are or *what* they do! According to J. P. Morgan's guideline, if the full-time equivalent salary of the average employee is $50,000 a year, then the top executive(s) should not earn more than $1,000,000. If someone has a problem making ends meet with a million bucks a year, then perhaps they frankly need to reevaluate their lifestyle. On the other hand, perhaps they should evaluate how their lowest-paid employees manage living on *their* income, which is often less than the above example.

Money, greed, and materialism stand to destroy the world. It's come down to the relatively few with millions and billions of dollars on one side, and the vast majority financially struggling to make ends meet on the other. Unfortunately, the middle class is slowly but surely joining the ranks of those struggling, with many wallowing in debt beyond their means.

If people would work at improving human relations as hard as they work at obtaining material possessions and status, the world would be a far better place. Unfortunately, we continue bad habits. Money and power have blinded many with certain people becoming obsessed, often losing the ability to genuinely care about anyone else but themselves. Blinded by greed, as the old saying goes.

It was Albert Einstein who said, "*Try not to become a man of success but rather try to become a man of value.*"

Another popular and powerful statement says; *On your deathbed, you won't be wishing you had spent more time at the office.* Devoting most of one's time to taking care of business rather than relationships will leave people longing for something far more important they may have missed in life, no matter how much fame and fortune were acquired along the way.

It's most unfortunate that while climbing ladders of success, many end up living unprincipled lives. I personally don't think most people handle fame and fortune very well. After they reach a certain level of wealth, above and beyond what they feasibly need to be comfortable and secure, something strangely predictable begins to happen – it goes to their heads. I don't mean to stereotype, but a substantial number of the overly affluent have lost their humane senses. Many of them become high-profile personalities that don't seem to genuinely care about the rest of the world population out there beyond their own gated and guarded communities. Their superiority complexes and supremist perceptions over the nonaffluent masses are developed through snobby, high society cultures and peer pressures, and their financial and political powers dictate and control the general direction of the economy, allowing others to exist merely as the hired help. Thus, much of working blue-collar people are exploited and forced to live from paycheck to paycheck. Consequently, the rich inevitably get richer, by design, no matter what the state of the economy.

In example of these financial influences, we should look at the evolution of our society's mandated occupational health and safety programs. Both the Occupational Safety and Health Administration (OSHA) and State Workers' Compensation started out as fair systems aimed at caring for workers who became injured or ill while on the job, due to accidents and unsafe or unhealthy working conditions. They were, and still are, good systems by design but, in effect, resulted in padding the pockets of greedy medical, legal, and insurance professionals. With Workers' Compensation, employees, perhaps backed into financial corners, often may choose to defraud the system to pay for unaffordable and outlandish medical attention that they couldn't afford otherwise.

What these programs ultimately

accomplished was to raise the costs of employers doing business, resulting in further budget cutbacks and stagnant wages for average workers. Consequently, with this situation added to others, the cost of living keeps inflating, but wages often fail to keep up. Stand back and look at where all the money really goes, and whom it really benefits – not the average worker by any means. We've seen the same things happen with other systems like unions and unemployment compensation as well.

What we have, considering the people driving these systems, is the exploitation, or as NBC News called it, *The Fleecing of America.* Hardworking-class people are being subjugated – *fleeced.* The average individual pays for it every time they go shopping for overpriced products and services. Life doesn't have to be so expensive, but it is.

So, where has all the money gone? Just look at the number of multimillion-dollar secondary homes (mansions) that exist throughout prestigious resort areas, like the Aspen home sold for ten million dollars by Enron's Kenneth Lay, the former CEO of Enron, who was convicted on multiple counts of fraud and conspiracy related to the company's collapse. Unfortunately, many people can't afford *any* home, let alone multimillion-dollar vacation homes. That said, there are hundreds of thousands of homeless people throughout America. As a tragic example of the severity of this situation, I can remember local news reports of a homeless sixty-year-old woman found huddled in a refrigerator-sized cardboard box one cold January winter morning, dead from exposure. And there are affluent people heating their giant vacation homes when they aren't even occupied.

Have we become that much of an irresponsible, uncaring society?

You may ask, just what could or should we be doing about it? Charles Birch said it best when he emphasized, *"The rich must live more simply, so that the poor may simply live."*

As I've mentioned, with all due respect, there *are* some very responsible, wealthy people on this planet, like Warren Buffett, considered the darling of business ethics and success, and who co-founded The Giving Pledge with Bill and Melinda Gates, asking billionaires to commit to giving away over half their wealth to charity, with Buffett himself pledging more than 99% of his wealth to philanthropic foundations. So, it *is* possible to be both rich *and* ethical too. In that respect, we have to be careful not to stereotype all rich people.

As for unprincipled wealthy people who are not ethically responsible, I know of a multimillionaire who also had a mansion near Vail, Colorado, who gained his wealth in a scam by ripping off senior citizens of their lifelong savings and retirement funds. He eventually got caught, but I'm sure he wasn't detained long, provided he was able to afford the best lawyers available.

Another universal principle of managing life: *Money doesn't buy happiness*. Living a principle-centered life and assuming responsibilities to community, family and friends are far more important values and should never be abandoned or neglected in the pursuit of fame and fortune.

By the time we become adults, we should learn to be unselfish and to take ethical responsibility, no matter what the situation or relationship. It's the key to true happiness, but it mostly stems from and depends upon our upbringing.

Whether they realize and admit it or not, many adults are too often remiss at taking responsibility while never fully growing up. Frankly, not that any of us are perfect, but some of the most irresponsible and immature people I know are merely grownup kids. I'm sure you know a few of them yourself. In fact, a lot of adults, for example, tend to act like children when shifting blame or throwing temper tantrums just to get their way. Even politicians tend to lie and deny when it comes to their wrongdoings.

So, why is it that many so-called mature adults can't face up to responsibility? One reason might be that in a free society, people have the ability to act *irresponsible*, that is, unless they have learned and have been instilled with ethical principles from childhood. Additionally, certain people have acquired inflated egos, which continually need to be fed with power. If all adults could learn and actually manage to set their egos aside and take responsibility, morally and ethically, for their own actions, the world would be a better place for everyone, including them.

Granted, there *are* people who do act responsibly, but many more do not. We should be able to open any phone book to find a limited number of listings for *ethical* lawyers that deal with taxes, estates, and other legitimate, professional legal matters – private *or* public. Instead, we find Yellow Page after Yellow Page of personal-injury professionals and lawyers specializing in all types of individual and class-action litigation, just itching to run to our sides in the name of *justice*. Why? There's big money in it. Who cares if it's ethical or responsible? Not to stereotype lawyers, but more often than not, many are merely seeking to make more than just their next BMW payment, or their country-club dues. Many of them really couldn't care less about you or me as human beings, but rather, what our unfortunate situations can do for them.

Many law school graduates go into politics and some are elected to State Legislatures and Congress as lawmakers. We've all witnessed the irresponsibility coming out of those bodies.

Then, there is the presidency of the United States as the top political position in the entire Free World. To its discredit, there have been some immoral and less-than-responsible things going on around the oval office in the past and present. Ego and the lack of taking ethical responsibility go all the way to the top.

Outside of the public and political arenas, people stop taking responsibility in their own personal lives too. Adults have now reached the point where more of us are divorced than not. According to the U.S. Census Bureau, almost twenty million American adults per year were being divorced at the turn of this last century. Consequently, so many children are being raised in single-parent or no-parent broken homes. According to the county records where I live, divorces outnumbered marriages by a margin of two to one. I'm afraid that situation would be comparable in many other areas across America as well.

Couples not taking responsibility for sacred marriage vows are usually the cause of irreconcilable differences or indifferences that lead to divorce. Each side's biased perception of the situation at hand will most always point an accusing finger at the other. Again, the ability to take responsibility in life begins with one's instilled values from childhood – seemingly the heart of many social problems.

Considering personal relationships, responsibility is not only restricted to romantic and marital interactions. There is a responsibility also involved any time two or more individuals enter business, organizational, or social affiliations.

It can be argued that anyone can walk away from relationships any time they feel like it, for whatever reasons; it's their right to do so. True, technically they can, but there are responsible ways to do that, should either of the parties decide to end the partnership. Merely getting tired of the situation, without good cause, and conveniently running away and avoiding it, or walking out on it without attempting to resolve the dissension, doesn't constitute responsibility. In every case, when responsibility is avoided, someone will get hurt. Rejection and abandonment are the most powerful psychological weapons ever deployed by humanity. There are many adults in the world who are guilty of resorting to these tactics. Sadly, when it comes to broken homes, these social weapons too often effect innocent children in the process.

In these situations, the inflicting individuals will often callously claim *they'll get over it,* but *they* rarely do, especially the children, and the resulting damage just accumulates with time, transforming itself into deep-seated forms of denied love which can result in anger. This anger unavoidably transitions itself into various forms of other undesirable behaviors, resulting in further social complications.

Ultimately, any human relationship, simple or committed, is extremely fragile and can be irreparably shattered and destroyed if not handled carefully and responsibly. Having this knowledge, it is therefore our obligation to actively practice trustworthiness and dependability in our personal relationships.

To paraphrase a simple golden rule or universal principle that has been around for centuries, it basically says, *Be as responsible with others as you'd expect them to be responsible with you.* Ironically, irresponsible people often develop grudges against responsible people for holding *them* responsible. After a while, trustworthy people can't help but to get discouraged and disgusted while having to deal with these types of individuals. The problem is, irresponsible people can't seem to see through their biased perceptions and opinions. If they could, they might change their actions to be more responsible.

One pet peeve I have related to being responsible adults is, you guessed it, *pets.* From dogs at large and uncontrolled barking, to harassing wildlife and not picking up poop; if you can't be a responsible pet owner, you shouldn't own pets.

Another peeve involving irresponsible and inconsiderate adults would be highway driving. In increasingly dense traffic conditions, some drivers have resorted to road rage, acknowledging each other with middle fingers, curses, and sometimes deadly weapons. Without self-discipline and respect for others, people sometimes lose control of their behaviors while endangering the lives of others who share the road with them. Irresponsible as they are, most inconsiderate situations involving motorists don't compare to the following true story:

There was a disturbed woman standing on the edge of a major highway overpass in Seattle, threatening to jump. The situation had developed into quite a spectator event with traffic backed up for miles while authorities attempted to coax the woman away from the edge. Many of the motorists had grown impatient after being held up in traffic for so long, so they started chanting for the woman to jump. Well…she did. Do you suppose these people would have encouraged her to jump if she had been their own sister or mother? It just proves the level of incivility and lack of care that sometimes exists in our society.

Yet another gripe is people being allowed to abuse the bankruptcy laws. NBC News reported that at the turn of this last century, there were around 1,550,000 people filing for bankruptcy each year, by far the highest level in history at the time. That's hardly a responsible way to get rid of your financial problems. Let's go out and spend as much money as we can on credit, until we can't possibly pay it all back. Then, we'll just walk away from our debts and let others pay for it. Just like all the garbage along the highways – out of personal sight, out of mind. Let somebody else clean it up. Perhaps financially irresponsible people who carelessly claim bankruptcy should be required to work it off, at minimum wage, by picking up garbage along the roadsides.

Sorry, I guess I just don't believe in allowing people to walk away from the messes *they* create while the rest of society has to roll up their sleeves and clean it up. There's no excuse for it, except to blame it on a lack of responsibility, more than likely brought about by, as we keep seeing, a lack of self-discipline and integrity.

On the other hand, with credit-card bankruptcy, I have to say that much of the blame falls on the creditors themselves. Substantial (four figure) credit amounts should never be extended to anyone without collateral, especially teenagers and young adults who haven't previously and fully proven their financial responsibility. Additionally, do the banks really need to charge so much interest? Tragically, there have been actual situations where young people have committed suicide over their out-of-control credit balances. In these situations, the creditors might shoulder as much blame as the borrowers. Furthermore, as long as the terms were reasonable, the principal balance should never actually be cancelled and should be the responsibility of the debtor, along with a fair payment plan. Let's just hope the bankruptcy laws eventually change and that the predatory lenders (loan sharks) and greedy creditors manage to clean up their acts.

Another universal principle of managing

life, and an obvious sound financial policy, simply states; *Don't spend more than you earn!*

Responsibilities follow us everywhere, even into the bedroom. Speaking for my generation back in the 1970s, I don't think many young adults, especially of college age, knew the meaning of the term *responsible sex*. *Free love* was more the norm. I believe it still would be if sexually transmitted diseases (STDs) hadn't come along and spoiled the party for everyone. Obviously, sexual promiscuity, along with variations of sexual orientation, played a significant role in the spread of STDs. Could nature have been putting up a red flag, giving us a warning? I really don't think Mother Nature, when she created and evolved human beings, intended for people to get their signals crossed. As for the natural purpose of sexual organs, they've been perfectly designed for a specific reproductive reason. When we try to make exceptions and variations, things start to go awry.

Today, with civilized societies mostly shying away from free love due to the risks, the moral focus has since shifted to sexual orientation. I tend to believe that natural principles dictate that sexual functions are meant to take place in a natural manner and that abnormal variations are not only unnatural but may also be unhealthy. However, I would like to emphasize that one of the last prejudices that need to be confronted by society is that against LGBTQ orientations.

Wrong or right, they are a personal choice of those who practice them and, in principle, should not be discriminated against.

In all fairness to the LGBTQ community, just like the preprogrammed tendency to fight or flight in a violent society, or like genetic mental illnesses, certain sexual orientations may have inherited a condition that is out of their own personal control. Professionals in genetics and psychology now feel there could likely be a gene associated with sexual orientation and that one may be born with this predisposition. If that is the case, then society should learn to end its prejudice against it. Like mental illness, certain cases of sexuality, moral or not, may be hardwired into the biological and mental makeup of many of the people that it inflicts. So, we should not prejudge people for conditions and dispositions that may genetically be out of their own personal control. To do so is no different than prejudging them for the color of their inherited skin or hair.

There are many areas of life about which we have little knowledge. Until we have a better understanding of things, we should stick to the basics of mutual respect and civility. Even though we may disagree with each other, we should at least agree to disagree in a genuinely polite manner. Engaging in heated arguments or violence with someone over different values than your own is neither a responsible or *wise choice*. Respectful personal conduct *is* a choice we humans need to come to grips with. It's not that hard to smile and be kind to others. *Now, be nice!* That's a phrase our mothers taught us, but one that some people seem to have a hard time putting into practice. Why can't we all be civil with each other? What is it that keeps us from it? Anger? Fear? Jealousy? Any of these negative symptoms, among others, again point to a lack of instilled character.

These behavioral symptoms are quite prevalent when dealing with prejudice and diversity in our society. When we deliberately put down others because they are different from ourselves, if not for spite, is it not at least partially out of fear that they may pass us up or take something away from us? As individuals, we may be so afraid of others who threaten our personal lifestyles, freedoms, or level of status that we develop prejudice against them and sometimes, hatred toward them, even if we don't know them personally.

Recently, the science of management has recognized the true value of diversity and unity in our personal and professional lives. If the nations and the peoples of the world could drop their prejudice, stop fighting, and work together as a team, we could sooner solve a lot of our major problems such as famine, disease, and pollution. I'm reminded of a quote by C. William Pollard, who said, "*Diversity without unity makes about as much sense as dishing up flour, sugar, water, eggs, shortening, and baking powder on a plate and calling it a cake.*"

Too many people have resisted putting the required amount of socially effective ingredients into what amounts to tasteless human relations.

In relation to human relations and diversity, I always thought that diverse music appreciation may actually be a gauge of unprejudiced behavior. I feel a person's ability to appreciate diverse types of good music is directly proportionate to their ability to appreciate diverse types of good people. The key word here being *good* in both cases.

In summary, while attempting to make a point, I have cited within this chapter many examples of social and material irresponsibility throughout our adult society. That point being, we so-called responsible adults are often much less responsible than we may think we are. Many people can't seem to take responsibility for their own actions, for very simple and selfish reasons. Due to the lack of ethics and self-discipline, many people are obviously unable to govern and manage themselves without perceptional and biased arguments continually arising. To again quote one of my favorite authors, Steven Covey, who says, "*When managing in the wilderness of the changing times, a map is of limited worth. What's needed is a moral compass.*" The concept Covey described is that people and organizations, to include governments, are not fully following a compass that always points toward ethics and responsibility. That compass will always, unquestionably, point to that true north, keeping us from going south in our lives – provided we have the self-discipline and morality to follow its direction.

After witnessing the state of this union for decades, I would suggest that perhaps our society might go back to square one and take another look at that compass. If we're ever going to get our act together and rid ourselves of the dysfunctional problems we have, it's time we take them seriously.

Historically, there was a similar situation that destroyed another affluent world civilization. America has been compared to ancient Rome.

According to Gore Vidal, who authored *The Decline and Fall of the American Empire*, fashioned after Edward Gibbon's *The Decline and Fall of the Roman Empire*, Vidal wrote, *"On September 16, 1985, when the Commerce Department announced that the United States had become a debtor nation, the American Empire died."* He went on to say, *"Like most modern empires, ours rested not so much on military prowess as on economic primacy."* Selfish greed and corruption have all but destroyed that primacy.

When you look closely at the circumstances, many Americans are presently following an uncanny parallel path that caused the fall of the Roman Empire. That being:

Immoral and indecent behavior, injustice, rottenness, greed, and malice; they are full of envy, murder, wrangling, treachery, and spite as well as libelers, slanderers, rude, arrogant and boastful, enterprising in evil, rebellious to parents, without brains, honor, love, or pity. Aware of their wrongdoings, yet they not only do it but even applaud others who do the same.

That writing is from a letter to the Romans from St. Paul, taken from the New Testament. Rome, after rising, most assuredly did eventually fall to the unsuspecting character and dismay of the Romans themselves; they also were obviously not following any moral compass at the time. The Romans were well advised within the scriptures but failed to read and follow the compass out of the woods.

Will America find its way out of the woods?

The compass is still there, as it has always been. And it still undeniably points to true north. Clearly, if it's ever going to happen, it's our *responsibility* as a society, and as individuals *of* that society, to read it and follow it. No one else *can* or *will* take that responsibility for us.

Ultimately, with enough knowledge and wisdom, grown people do have the ability to transform themselves into *responsible adults*.

Middle Ages

A Pirate Looks at Forty

— Jimmy Buffet

By the time we reach the age of forty, we may begin to pay more attention to the fact that most people fit into one of the following categories when it comes to marital or nonmarital status. Either they're single and relatively young, say under the age of thirty, in which case, it's pretty easy to interact and socialize with friends and acquaintances, especially in your own age group. Or, they find themselves married, young or old, without kids, whereby they can, at least, mutually entertain each other with annoying personal habits. Or, ideally fulfilling the *American Dream,* they're happily married with perfect careers, two or three perfect kids, living in a perfect neighborhood and a perfect house, with a late-model SUV or two, a dog, a cat, and goldfish. Many may make it to this category, but all too often, something can still go missing...happiness.

To their misfortune, with the skyrocketing divorce rate, the middle-aged might find themselves living outside of *any* dream, suddenly single again, with jobs they don't particularly care for, not-so-perfect kids, in a less-than-perfect neighborhood, driving an older vehicle that's frequently in need of repairs. Or, heaven forbid, they find themselves at this age with no immediate family and no social life, to the point they wished they had anyone to talk to other than telephone solicitors, in which case, they may need a few good books, television with several hundred channels, along with an Internet connection.

Being middle-aged and single, hanging out in the bars and crashing parties is no longer much of a realistic or responsible option. After forty, social functions can become fewer and farther between, compared to the availability and variety of them back in their twenties and thirties – especially if they're not much of a social butterfly or party animal. Many, faced with this predicament in this fast-paced, high-tech world, have gone into cyberspace to hang out, meet other people, and to socialize. After all, people can only carry-on conversations and arguments with their pets for so long. Adding to that, family and friends may not be there for them socially anymore, as they once may have been, at least not on a regular basis. So, one has to do whatever works; and in this day and age, computers are becoming the growing medium for communicating and socializing. However, like the real world, people still have to be careful and cautious, since many other middle-aged singles may be single for good reasons.

Unfortunately, due to declining ethics in

the world today, people can become disappointed and hurt just as much while cyber-socializing as they can the old-fashioned way. Not being face-to-face with the ability to look others in the eye, or to be able to read body language, computers have unfortunately made it much more convenient for people to be dishonest and pretentious with each other, and many people who use personal ads for dating are already married. That says something about the level of integrity in the world today.

I suppose the main advantage of singles using computers to socialize is that they have access to a greater variety of people. And with today's sophisticated databases, one can even do selective searches and screenings for the exact type of person one is looking for, that is, as long as people *are* being truthful and unpretentious. As I indicated, pretension and dishonesty may end up being the weak link in the whole system. Hopefully, this doesn't ruin it for everyone.

As for myself, a hopeless romantic, I have to say that I prefer the old-fashioned, more personal way of meeting people. After all, it's a small world, and I truly believe that if you're in the right places at the right times, you'll cross paths with the right people. But there could be a catch to that – you may need to have full, undiluted faith in destiny for that to magically happen.

As far as unprincipled expectations go in the modern dating arena, it seems men in general are frivolously attracted to women with fine figures that could model swimsuits for *Sports Illustrated*. In the same way, too many women seem to be overly infatuated with *tall, dark, and handsome*, not to mention *rich and famous*. Due to the influence of unrealistic media, like magazines, movies, and romance novels that we're all exposed to, I think people's expectations have become a little skewed and impractical. It seems that traits such as intelligence and integrity often take a back seat to characteristics like vanity and financial success.

In any case, if you find yourself middle-aged and single, you might be asking yourself just how you ended up there. For some, it could have happened after experiencing the challenges of a midlife crisis followed by divorce.

Certain people during the midlife phase may take up all sorts of strange hobbies and pastimes, like wealthy adventurers who spend a considerable amount of their time and fortunes attempting to break world records at extreme activities. I'm afraid some people have far too much time and money on their hands. These adventurers may have succeeded at breaking world records, but were any of these time-consuming and expensive feats actually productive? Did any of them contribute to society or act to solve the world's most crucial problems, or were they just aimed at providing personal thrills and inflating egos?

Others going through this phase of midlife,

like all of those married people using personal ads, might go so far as to have an extramarital affair just for the sheer excitement. Unfortunately, once the initial excitement and novelty have worn off, affairs often have a way of dangerously backfiring.

Any way you look at it, it seems that people in the Free World, especially America, are not easily or inexpensively entertained these days. Once again, it could have something to do with the way they were raised. A prime example would be the widespread problem Americans (including kids) now have with weight control, as witnessed by the slew of over-advertised, deceiving testimonials and dietary guarantees in the media today. That sensational product, as seen as on TV. The amazing breakthrough in weight loss that not only burns fat, but increases energy, and controls appetite as well.

Many Americans have personally allowed themselves to become obese, killing themselves from the inside out, especially middle-aged Americans, where sedentary lifestyles are commonplace and where metabolisms and levels of exercise have slowed to a snail's pace. Mind you, I'm not talking about people that unfortunately may have inherited metabolism problems through genetics, for which there are new medical revolutions for that. I'm talking about people that frankly have little-to-no willpower when it comes to maintaining a healthy lifestyle to include diet and exercise.

According to the American Heart Association, obesity among Americans, both young and old, has increased at an alarming rate in recent years. The fact of the matter, being overweight is not healthy. It can lead to critical problems such as diabetes, high blood pressure, and heart disease, just to name a few. The medical community has warned that if this trend continues, obesity will overtake smoking as the nation's leading cause of preventable death.

We should learn to listen to our bodies and minds as well as our doctors. Of all the times that I've either eaten too much or drank too much, it has never left me feeling well, emotionally *or* physically. That brings us to yet another universal principle of life: *With the exception of love – everything should be taken in moderation.* We should learn to fill ourselves with *affections* instead of confections.

When it comes to maintaining weight, people have to train their minds to make *wise choices* as a matter of self-discipline. They need to develop healthy eating habits and learn to exercise more. That's usually all there is to it, and it doesn't drain your budget. In fact, you can actually save money by eating right, since healthy foods are usually cheaper than junk foods. You'll also save money on medical bills because your health will improve. Additionally, you don't have to join any expensive health clubs – walking or running is free. If not for yourself, do it for your loved ones. All it takes is a little self-discipline, hopefully taught and learned early on. Fortunately, if you didn't learn it as a child, it's never too late. Making tough choices, although difficult, will strengthen your ability to discipline yourself.

Considering unhealthy consumer habits, when the economy is experiencing tough times, certain companies actually do rather well; like tobacco company Philip Morris, and alcohol distributors like Diageo and Anheuser-Busch. In a bad economy, certain vices remain quite profitable.

With middle age, there are many options and scenarios for dealing with this particularly stressful period in one's life. For some, they may find themselves going back to school. Perhaps this is one of the most sensible options, however, it's not the easiest or most affordable, especially with a full-time career and family to consider.

For me, being in my early 40s, the first year or so of graduate school was great, since I was invigorated and wrapped up in this newfound midlife challenge. However, by the last year of it, I was ready to wrap it up. By then, I was on a first-name basis with some of the convenient-store clerks along I-70 in the mountain towns of Colorado, between Denver and Vail, where I frequently stopped for coffee and food while commuting to and from school at Regis University in Denver. On top of working an average of fifty hours a week at my job in Vail, this academic routine soon wore out its welcome.

My wife put up with the situation fairly

well, I thought, but we apparently had grown further apart in the process, because shortly after I graduated, she packed up and moved out. She left for no cardinal reason other than what she may have perceived as my not being there for her anymore. Like many men, I suppose I was considered to be insensitive.

With all due respect to women, men are sometimes unfairly accused of not understanding or not being sensitive to women's needs. I'm afraid it goes much deeper than that. As I see it, social standards and early conditioning are the primary influences at the heart of that problem.

Historically, due to highly competitive and *macho* cultures in our society, it has not been socially acceptable for men to display emotion or sensitivity. Society and parents, for generations, have stressed to their sons from early childhood, *big boys don't cry*. So, boys grow up and are often considered to be *weak* if they display sensitive emotions. Yet, in this modern world, women want men to be sensitive, along with big and strong. Unfortunately, the deeply ingrained program to be *insensitive* will often overpower and outstrip any conscious attempt to be *sensitive*. It becomes a real catch-22 at times.

What to do? "*Mammas, don't let your babies grow up to be cowboys.*" In other words, parents need to stop telling their sons, *big boys don't cry,* that is, if they want them to be sensitive with women when they grow up. Otherwise, they may end up not only cowboys, but also *desperados*.

So, I'll admit, men are, in fact, guilty of being insensitive, at least to a certain degree, but the road goes both ways. In that respect, each gender needs to at least try to understand the other before they insensitively pass judgment.

Letting everyone in on yet another universal principle of managing life, involving some of the psychology behind self-discipline that I learned while studying management, and that we all need to actively pay more attention to in our lives:

You cannot directly change or control the actions of others; you can only change your own actions, and then, only if it becomes personally important enough for you to do so.

With awareness and persistence, like quitting a bad habit, sometimes through crisis, you can personally change, but don't drive yourself and everyone else around you crazy trying to change others. That is especially true when it comes to your spouse. If you genuinely love and/or respect the people around you, it's okay to tactfully and diplomatically communicate your concerns with them, but don't go so far as to destroy the relationship. You'd be better served by developing your own communicative skills, while slowly raising your level of awareness of your loved ones' feelings. Over time, if they come to appreciate and respect your opinions, then perhaps they'll eventually feel compelled to slowly change themselves more to your liking. That, however, is the only way anyone can indirectly effect lasting change in others – through the power of genuine care and respect, topped off with a little kindness and, of course, trust. Combined, it is the glue, or principles, that hold relationships together.

Related to individuals trying to change the world, I was substitute teaching a freshman high school math class one day with several obviously angry and emotionally disturbed kids as my students. With their regular teacher not there, they started drawing antigovernment, antiestablishment, as well as anti-everyone else (different from them) symbols and slogans all over the whiteboards, instead of doing the algebra assignment for that day. So, with that, I explained to them that their concerns were valid, but they should not drive themselves and everyone else around them crazy, trying to change the world with negative sentiments. I further explained that they would be better off concentrating more *positive* efforts within their own circles of influence. For that, they just gave me a bunch of disinterested anti-substitute-teacher looks. I asked them to at least think about it, to erase the boards, and to do their algebra. From my own knowledge and experience, I knew I wasn't about to instantly change their minds and attitudes. Hopefully, some of it sunk in though.

Divorce often follows folks into midlife. One of the problems in the world today, for many people, is that *for better or for worse* really doesn't mean much. In most cases, what do you think is the primary cause of divorce? If you said money, you're close, even though money happens to be a primary reason or *excuse* given by people for divorce. However, even with the disagreement over finances ranking supposedly at the top of most marital difficulties, it's merely a symptom of the real problem.

If you said sex, you're also close, since sex, or the lack thereof, happens to be another most common excuse for divorce. Here again, nonfunctional sex is also only a symptom of the real problem.

Frankly speaking, whether or not anyone wants to admit it, the primary cause of divorce boils down to *self-centeredness* – a characteristic weakness in people – contributed to a lack of genuine care for others. The jury is out and many of us are, in fact, guilty. Admit it, we *should* care, but we usually aren't all that concerned enough about others unless they happen to have something we want. All too often, we're just interested in what *they* can do for *us*, rather than what *we* could be doing for *them*. Thus, a primary root problem among humanity is the absence of inbred consideration - love and respect for others. It was Saint Paul who said:

"Love is patient and kind; love is not

jealous or boastful; it is not arrogant or rude. Love does not insist on its own way; it is not irritable or resentful; it does not rejoice at wrong, but rejoices in the right. Love bears all things, believes all things, hopes all things, endures all things."

The absence of genuine love and respect is unquestionably found at the heart of our relationship problems. If true love and respect existed, divergence would not.

The next thing on the list of contributing factors to the disparity among people is *lack of communication*. Communications, no doubt, has turned out to be one of the biggest challenges facing mankind. Be it in government, marriage, between friends, or in the workplace and other organizations; miscommunication is simply the result of what is *misarticulated* on one side versus what is *misperceived* on the other.

Considering these problems, if both sides would just *try* to see each other's viewpoints, then we wouldn't experience this gross communication breakdown that is affecting all levels of society. We'd then be faced only with simple disagreements. Most importantly, we need to remember that we are not our opinions, since opinions can be changed.

All in all, most human interactions are either facilitated in the right direction with good communication skills or are torn in conflict by a lack *of* them. Have you ever felt like you were having a good conversation with someone when they abruptly exclaimed, "*I disagree!*" Just like that? Frankly, those kinds of opinionated expressions do nothing to facilitate further open communication. Instead, people would be far more effective communicators by simply saying; *That's an interesting viewpoint...I'm not sure...you know what I think?* It's only good manners to ask instead of tell. This communicative approach is far more politically positive and will command further communication and respect. They may even intently listen to what you have to say!

So much for Effective Communication 101 that we hopefully learn to practice and teach to others, especially children, by the time we reach middle age.

Often, during midlife crises, while failing to get values in order, there are some highly unfriendly legal systems that adults may unfortunately experience. Sometimes drugs and alcohol become a crutch to get through ugly situations, which can lead to irresponsibly running away from life and setting bad examples to those who would otherwise look up to us. Many of us have been there; some never return to reality. For example, following their arrest for driving under the influence (DUI), people can find themselves appearing in court numerous times, paying thousands of dollars in legal fees and fines, attending drug-and-alcohol-awareness classes, and having their driver's licenses revoked. Then there's all of the community service they get sentenced to, not to mention having their auto insurance premium skyrocket to the maximum limit for the next five years. In these situations, instead of *facing* their problems and solving them, some people continue to run away from them, creating even bigger problems. In the end, the lawyers and, perhaps, the insurance companies are the only ones that really benefit from this dysfunctional process.

So, how do we repair core values at middle age? The best way *not* to fix the problem is through punitive and uncaring legal systems. This flies in the face of modern management theory. *Corrective measures*, to include education, are the most effective approach. With proper management, society can plan, organize, direct, and control *desired* behaviors, so that it doesn't find itself having to punish or futilely trying to alter *undesirable* behaviors. Ideally, this process best takes place, while growing up, through effective child rearing, but it is possible for people to change at any phase of life.

When parenting fails, the people often produced from it don't need to be dragged through additional emotional mud and further psychological slime. Strictly *punishing* people may be adding fuel to a fire that caused their dysfunctional behavior in the first place. That may lead to further financial and/or psychological complications causing even bigger problems, possibly sending them over the edge of despair. Driven there by the system, these people may very well pose an even *greater* threat to society than they ever did before. At that point, all you can do is lock them up and throw away the key – not a very responsible solution to a fairly preventable problem.

To those people who callously say, *Tough Twinkies, they* (meaning the guilty as charged) *should have thought about that beforehand,* I would say, *Let's get real.* How can people with weak integrity be completely blamed for a problem that they personally didn't create? Ultimately, due to generations of bad guardianship, it's *everyone's* fault, though we all still have to individually take responsibility for it. As a civilized society dealing with these situations, let's not go so far and be so callous as to further destroy what may already be fragile lives. We should reach out and seriously attempt to fix these problems through *correctional* measures, especially with first-time offenders. Using positive corrective and educational measures to alter behavior, rather than strict punishment alone, makes the most sense. More importantly, *prevention* becomes the process whereby we actually tackle the root problems before they become lost causes. Currently, many of the legal systems in our society are too quick to *kick them when they're down,* rather than support these offenders, while helping them get up and get through their dilemmas, to hopefully not make the same mistakes again. Why should the answer to people's chronic personal problems have to end with a swift kick in the butt, along with the message; *Shape up or ship out?* Obviously, that approach is not working very well.

Further tackling the root problems, I strongly feel that people need to be thoroughly trained and licensed before they are ever allowed to become parents – just as much, if not more than drivers or pilots. Furthermore, they should have to requalify and renew their parenting licenses periodically, until their children are fully grown. I truly believe this to be an extremely important process for society to consider. Otherwise, like misguided vehicles or aircraft, people risk crashing and burning their lives, as well as other lives. As an added benefit, with more knowledgeable and skilled parents guiding their children into principle-centered adulthood, society might not require quite as many legal or law enforcement professionals in the future. Conclusively, parenting is not only an art, but also a science that requires a lot of knowledge, experience, and skill, all aided by and needing education.

Right after Columbine, while in my mid-forties, after experiencing some undesirable challenges of midlife myself, including divorce, I followed a new direction and became reoccupied as a writer, teacher, and consultant.

When I first started teaching in the public schools, I assumed that with my age, experience, and education, I would likely be placed at the high school level where I really wanted to observe teenagers. As fate would have it, my first day on the job as a sub, I was given the first grade in elementary school. I'll admit, this was a new experience. Virtually, overnight, I acquired the responsibility for an entire room full of six-year-olds, all sitting there, staring at me, as if to say; *What are you going to teach us?*

It wasn't long before the sugarcoated cereal they had consumed earlier that morning kicked in. I might add that the only time you can get twenty or more first graders who are under the influence of sweets to quiet down, is to plug in a popular children's video. Even at that, they will still squirm. When the video ended, the little volcanoes once again erupted. How can I describe these kids? Excitable? Yep. Noisy? Uh-huh. Making messes and not listening to anything being said to them? Well, I guess when it comes to that, first graders aren't unlike big people.

Teaching first grade was an experience. It appears to be true that people have already started to settle into their dominant personalities at that age. Genetics can be a factor, but lifestyle and upbringing, early on, is a primary influence. For example, happy, expressive kids, more often than not, are brought up in similar or complementary family structures and situations. It's the quiet, unhappy kids, or the mean, loud brats and bullies that we need to be concerned about.

As an inexperienced first-grade sub, but with professional training and experience in management psychology, it became clear to me that each of these kids reflected one of the four major personality styles namely, *driver*, *expressive*, *analytical*, or *amiable*.

One of the *drivers* kept handing me the bell from the teacher's desk, telling me I should ring it if I wanted the class to behave and quiet down, which didn't seem to always work.

Judging by the decibel level achieved by twenty first graders in the same room, I judged that most of these kids were *expressive*. However, I suppose the kid who came up and handed me a dripping-wet watercolor portrait of me, with my nickname, *Coop*, painted in the lower corner, was one of the true expressive impressionists of the group.

The *analyticals* headed straight for the computer, or anything techie.

During the course of the day, one of the *amiables* came up to me and gave me a big hug, but then became embarrassed and scurried off back to her desk with a gleeful grin and red face. All in all, despite putting up with a little whining and tattling off and on, I must say it was one of the most enlightening and entertaining days I've ever spent.

Young children are amazing! They're mostly unspoiled, eager to learn, and enthusiastic about life – traits that seem to wane as they evolve into adolescents. As a sad exception, I remember one little girl in that class who had already settled in to a quiet, unhappy personal state. She kept latching on to me, wanting my attention and affection. When I asked the school administration office about her, I discovered that she was being raised without full-time parents available, by a relatively young, single grandmother. Something was definitely missing from this little girl's life.

No matter the grade level, in addition to the structured curricula teachers have to follow, along with all of the duties and responsibilities they have, as well as the vast types of behaviors they must effectively cope with, they should be far more valued by society.

With all of the challenges that teachers face today, many children will arrive at school lacking solid character. Consequently, these kids require instruction in areas where their parents have failed.

I also believe business managers should have to teach grade school for at least a day, as human resource management training, prior to taking the reins of any professional organization. If you can manage grade school kids, you're off to a good start in understanding group dynamics and human relations.

Where would professionals, including

business leaders, come from if it were not for teachers? Conversely, who is it we value most in our society, and for what reason? Nonsensically, we put teachers near the bottom of the list of professions, way below highly valued occupations such as politicians, business managers, sports figures, and entertainers.

Midlife crises, at the time they're happening, can definitely be unnerving. However, I now clearly see them as valuable and necessary learning experiences that act to teach us critical lessons in life. Should we fail to stop and take heed of the underlying messages these experiences present to us, then we will undoubtedly fail to change and improve ourselves in the process, whereby we simply fail at the whole purpose of mastering life itself.

It was Mike McKinley who said, *"When we fail to change, we fail."*

For me, I now believe that my own learning experiences and the resulting changes have been a continuous transformation of my life from what it used to be, to what it has become, and to what it will become in the future. With these changes, aided by unforeseeable crises, I strongly believe that I have been spiritually guided and am thankfully headed in a more positive direction in life. Additionally, without the scope and magnitude of these life crises, I probably would have never written this book. In the process, I feel I was able to strengthen certain principles, such as integrity, patience and self-discipline, while at the same time weakening negative traits like anger, ego, and prejudice.

While learning, experiencing, and mastering life, there was a point in my career while working at Vail Resorts when I had the privilege of creating a national apprenticeship program for aerial tramway mechanics through the U.S. Department of Labor. From that opportunity, I experienced the very same growth process. That is, apprentices learn from the masters how to do what is required and to do things the *right* way. Then, they continue doing things under strict supervision until it's fully learned and consistently done correctly thereafter. Finally, they complete the cycle, thereby changing roles and becoming the *teachers* themselves. And the cycle resumes all over again – a natural process and universal principle that has been going on for generations. From this, I now realize that life itself is an apprenticeship of trial and error from beginning to end. What is important is that we continually learn and improve in a positive direction toward mastering it. I've also learned that after experiencing the first half of life, where I found myself using my *back* in occupation more than my *brains*, my role eventually changed into teaching to others what I have learned. That, in part, became another one of my primary inspirations to write this book and offer my knowledge in service of others.

Getting over the hump, so to speak, after

serving my apprenticeship, I can see and understand the overall human relationship situation much more clearly. What we presently have in our society is not only *power struggles*, but also *impasses* due to unrealistic expectations, in addition to pretense and deception. This has since escalated to a universal mistrust, for the most part, and has thus evolved into an all-out stalemate between people, be it individuals, genders, organizations, religious sects, or even entire countries. Until we realistically lower our vain and materialistic expectations and stop deceiving each other, the world will never reach an optimal state. Untrustworthiness and the resulting apprehension among people that goes along with it could continue indefinitely unless we begin to take corrective measures to break that cycle.

As a fact of life and yet another common principle, what people really want most is that which they spend the majority of their time trying to get. That said, the populace needs to quit focusing on superficial *wants* and start focusing on realistic *needs;* one of which is unselfish giving, be it either of oneself or one's excess material possessions. What I'm implying is, don't waste all of your time and money on yourself. Learn and experience the joy of sharing, improving, and celebrating life with others who may be less fortunate.

Conclusively, while serving your own

apprenticeship in life, if you should find yourself a middle-aged, somewhat-humbled-from-adversity person, have faith. Hopefully, you were raised with enough self-discipline and patience to stay the course and not get too discouraged or impatient. Moreover, keep in mind another important universal principle of managing life: *Quantity does not make up for quality.*

Finally, as an extremely important part of mastering life, we all need to learn to knowingly *choose* to critically look at the world around us unselfishly and objectively with an open mind and not prejudge what we *think* we are observing. Once we learn to do that, we're almost there.

Senior Civilization

I Still Haven't Found What I'm Looking For

— U2

Before we know it, lurking around the corner, there's old age sneaking up on us. Obviously, we can't avoid it, so we may as well just face it gracefully. Above all, we need to remember to keep our sense of humor, even if we can't seem to remember anything else.

Unfortunately, certain aspects of old age are not very enjoyable. According to CBS News, one out of three nursing home residents in America are subject to physical, sexual, or verbal abuse. Most are subject to neglect. I would question the ethics of people that abuse others. I hope they realize that they themselves may end up in that position. There *is* such a thing called *karma*.

Our senior citizens deserve respect, not neglect. In general, seniors are quite valuable to us since they are the wisest people we know, for good reason. They've been around the block a time or two, and most have learned from their mistakes. After all, silver and white are the badges of experience.

When you're young and healthy, you look at the rest of your life, especially old age, as something in the distant future. However, by the time you get past midlife, you then find yourself starting to look at life in retrospect.

In our silver years, the early stages and phases of life seem much different than they did while experiencing them. If only we could go back and live our lives all over again with the knowledge and experience we've obtained over the years, we would avoid a lot of headaches *and* heartbreaks. Considering the whole process, though, I really don't think it's designed to work that way. I truly believe that people are meant to season with time.

To use a common analogy of the earth's natural seasons, as related to the seasoning stages of human life, all people come into the world on an equal plane and begin to grow in the *spring* of their lives. They continue to flourish throughout their *summer* and their most active existence. Once reaching the *autumn* of their lives, like leaves, people display individual and colorful changes, and finally, without exception, each inevitably returns to the earth in symbolic *winter*, making way for the next generation. Just as seasonable growth cycles become an all-important requirement in botanical processes, they also apply to human development. Accordingly, spring and summer are prerequisite stages to experiencing autumn and winter. This universal principle holds true for maple leaves as well as human beings. That's not to say that autumn and winter are not just as critical and important in the process as the early seasons. As a standard, I believe all things and their moments in time have purpose.

The average human life span has now reached almost eighty years in this new millennium of ours, whereas it was much less than that back in frontier days. As a result, the seasons of our lives are, in effect, lengthening. The *spring* years can now be looked upon as an expanding range between birth and approximately twenty years of age – the sprouting, rapid growth and quick learning phase. With people living longer, and education continuing to evolve at the rate it is, human intelligence cannot help but to also become further advanced as time progresses. Children today have definitely gained in intelligence, partially measured by IQ scores, compared to where *my* generation was back in the spring of *my* life. Sometimes you wouldn't know it by looking at or talking to them, but nevertheless, kids are definitely becoming more intelligent with each generation. That may inevitably give the youth of the world more power as time goes on, since knowledge is a realistic and viable form of power. However, there is no substitute for good-old-fashioned experience – *seasoning*. Knowledge *with* experience will always outweigh intelligence alone. It's called *wisdom*.

Continuing the seasonal analogy of life, *summer* signifies an age range between twenty and forty – the growing, flourishing, and maturing phase, which has also become a huge opportunity for civilization to further advance its level of knowledge and understanding of the world we live in. This range in age is capable of being the most productive and progressive, provided greed and corruption don't stand in the way of ethical progress, which in the past has been such a hindrance to humanity.

As life progresses, people between the age of forty and sixty are considered to be in the *autumn* of their lives – yearning for meaning, hopefully fulfilling and mostly mastering life while passing on their knowledge to less-experienced younger generations. This demographic age range equally becomes a key opportunity in our society, further aiding in the ability of humanity to continue to advance itself.

Just think about how much more technology and knowledge exist to challenge the present generations, compared to earlier ones, and what remarkable changes can we envision for those generations yet to come? It is undeniably mind-boggling. For example, personal computers didn't even exist when I began college back in the early 1970s. Only large mainframe IBM business computers with their bulky keypunch cards were around at that time. Personal computers didn't arrive on the scene until the early 1980s.

Additionally, look at the changes that have occurred in the last century relative to aeronautics and space travel. And how about the advances contributing to better living through chemistry and medical science? Why do you think we're all living so much longer now? I can't understand people who have little to no respect for science. They're called *anti-intellectuals.*

Like the early-morning opening of a flower, what great advancements in science and technology we have seen unfold in the world around us in a relatively short time.

On New Year's Day of 2001, the mayor of Detroit opened a time capsule that was left by the city's previous mayor in the year 1901. From a wondrous list of questions found in the capsule, one asked; *Were we now able to telephone foreign countries?* I would wager those who placed the capsule couldn't have imagined that we'd be able to instantaneously e-mail the other side of the world, 24/7, from a small mobile device carried around in our pocket.

Hang on to your hats, folks! With the advent of Artificial Intelligence (AI), who knows what's around the next corner? Like a rollercoaster reaching its peak, this ride could soon get wild and crazy. Let's just hope it's a highly progressive one and we stop hampering progress with religious, political, legal, and personal disputes.

Yes, indeed, the changes that have unfolded in the course of a century are truly amazing. Furthermore, one person alone could not have accomplished any of these wondrous transformations. It only happens when society puts its collective heads and backs together, working as a team, that these advancements in science and technology become reality. Now, if only the world's diverse global civilizations could work together in the same manner to solve our most threatening problems, we would then have a world that all of us could live upon in true peace and harmony. Unfortunately for the world, as I have pointed out as one of the biggest problems facing mankind, self-centered and biased politics, revolving around religion, money, and valuable resources, has historically hindered global teamwork. Those in power have not been genuinely concerned with the benefits of *all* people. Because of greed and corruption, war and destruction have always been there to counteract and deter or destroy positive progression. Think of what the world could have accomplished by putting all of the resources and energy used to fight each other into positive and productive efforts instead. By now, we could have completely eliminated many of the severe problems that currently face us. There comes a point where people must wisely choose to advance social responsibility past the point of politics.

What I'm implying is that people, including nations, must learn to genuinely listen to each other with open minds and open hearts while trying to sincerely solve differences through communication and negotiation, rather than irresponsible squabbling and physical violence. In that respect, we as a society *do* have a *choice*. However, we must make intelligent choices in a reasonable amount of time. My fear is that it will take a continuation of devastating national and world crises before things actually have a chance to change for the better, provided we don't destroy ourselves in the meantime. It doesn't take the wisdom of the elderly to see that we as a society, up until now, have been headed in precarious directions. For example, Middle East terrorists, world dictators, and biased politicians are currently throwing a wrench into the positive works of this planet. Democratic societies don't stand a chance of communicating and negotiating with these unreasonable and irresponsible assemblages of selfishness. Terrorists, dictators, and other similar, bad people are nothing more than ruthless individuals without ethics, incapable of responsible communication and negotiation with the rest of society. America isn't what it used to be. I fear for our democracy.

Without question, in a global economy, we must make *wise choices* to overcome our special interests and biases if we expect to survive, let alone thrive. People have to start acting ethically, with dedication and commitment, in the *world's* best interest, instead of self-centered *special* interests. It was Shakespeare who equated man's self-centeredness and lack of compassion to the *cold winds of winter*. Further, the Bhagavad Gita (2,500 years ago) stated, "*The world is imprisoned in selfish action.*" Little has changed.

Can America and the rest of the Free World get where it needs to be in time to turn things around?

Not without enough *wisdom*.

We can, I believe, overcome our problems with education and ethics, but it has to be a top priority at this point. The worst thing we can do, especially with climate change and global warming, is to sit around and politically debate the situation like a bunch of frogs in hot water while the temperature slowly rises around us. RIBBIT

According to the U.S. National Climatic Data Center, since 1976, averaged temperatures have risen at a rate of 1.2 degrees Fahrenheit per decade. Who can deny that the weather is consequently changing around us?

Considering the temporal and environmental problems at hand, there are highly lobbied politicians who would handle the world's energy crises with more big business as usual, further expanding fossil fuel exploration and energy production; *Drill, baby, drill.* That only serves the fossil fuel industry, along with other related businesses that feed off of it. It doesn't, however, serve mankind and planet Earth. Others, being more enlightened, prefer to solve this threatening problem through conservation and technology while discovering new sources of clean energy to replace the demand for hydrocarbons like oil and gas. I happen to strongly agree that technology is obviously the long-term solution to supporting the growing number of people. Irresponsibly continuing to just use up all of the world's expendable resources will inevitably only lead us into the cold darkness of crises.

With energy shortages and global warming, which side of the political arena do you think is wisely taking a stand for ethical management in the world's best interest rather than their own special interests? You be the judge. A society should never go so far as to put its economy ahead of the world and its threatened environment. To do so is to put greed above wisdom.

Again, my worst fear is that big business and the lust for profits will come first, causing humanity to be forced into further crises. If you saw the movie *Erin Brockovich*, based on a true story, it depicts one of many similar corporate situations in today's economy, where a utility company put profits above and beyond human life. We can no longer sit back and say that *it's only a movie*. Greed is real, and it is driving the world exactly where it's headed – into major crises. If we're not careful, we're going to allow special interests to destroy our precious environment to the point where *nobody* is going to be able to fix it, at *any* cost.

So, what can we personally do about it? Being a democratic and free society, we can all use a responsible rule of thumb when we vote in elections. That is, to research and study the issues to the best of our ability, using reliable sources of information. From that perspective, while using critical thinking skills to question everything, along with higher levels of understanding concerning the issues, we should cast our vote *objectively* in the best interest of the world, and not *subjectively* in any special interest, including our own. This responsibility rests upon *all* voters, young *or* old. Are people in the Free World currently making *wise choices* when they go to the polls? Some are. Many are not. Senior citizens, in most cases, are likely making the most informed decisions, provided they themselves have not been blinded by ideologies and self-interest. The rest of society should listen to the elderly. As the Native Americans have proven for generations, the minds of senior citizens are a valuable resource.

With senior citizens, life, as I've described, symbolically turns to *winter*. This is not to say that after sixty, life has to be colorless and cold, devoid of all further meaning. It does, however, mean that by then, we had better have our acorns gathered. What *that* means is that seniors should have reached a level of wisdom, to include common sense, over and above younger generations. Hopefully, they have also learned to devote themselves, upon retiring from professional careers, to mentoring and volunteering in service of others, while passing on some of that knowledge before they leave this world. My being at that stage in life, I try to do that.

There is no such thing as retirement. By design, it's merely a shifting of societal roles. Seniors, therefore, have a choice, as well as a responsibility, to continue contributing to society – either that or become a burden upon it.

In one of *my* contributing roles as a teacher, I

was once given an assignment by the local school district at the end of a school year to teach a three-day make-up class of a dozen or so underachieving eighth graders. These kids had less than suddenly found themselves lagging behind the rest of the class, as well as the world, to the point of being in jeopardy of repeating the eighth grade. So, I was assigned to instruct this intensified class, designed to get these kids over the hump, out of middle school, and on to high school.

The course of study was designed to teach a wide variety of academic disciplines over the three-day period. It centered on a central theme related to the misguided aspects of today's society, compared to the historic cultural values of the Navajo Native Americans. Whether these young people realized it or not, this class was aimed at the root of their personal problems.

Throughout the three days, they were required to read and study a novel written about a young Native American in the *spring* of *his* life. The young Navajo boy in the book was having a great deal of difficulty relating to and identifying with his elders. That included his very traditional Navajo grandfather, in the *winter* of *his* life, who, without question, was very wise. His grandfather, no doubt, better understood the world but was still somewhat mystified by the ways of modern society and its younger people.

Considering the context of this teaching assignment, I had a suspicion that these academically and socially challenged kids were coming from disrupted families, so, the first morning, I asked them to raise their hands if they were from broken homes. As I suspected, practically every hand in the room went up.

The breakdown of family, as I have dwelled upon throughout this book, is one of the primary causes of dysfunction as well as underachievement and trouble in our society.

As pointed out in the book required for this particular class, Native American culture was one where women historically ruled the home, becoming the matrix that held the rest of the family members together. The father's role was to show the boys how to hunt, fish, and compete among other tribes. They were supposed to be the breadwinners and protectors. The role of the elderly, as related to this chapter, was to supply crucial guiding *wisdom*. Those roles, put together, were gravely critical for survival.

In a similar situation, in more recent times, the Southern Ute Tribe, in the Four Corners area of the American Southwest, ousted its tribal chairman. This was due to the fact that this modern-minded Native American, even though college educated, would not listen to the wisdom of his tribal council elders and consequently risked his people's deep-rooted and long-proven cultural values. The same thing is happening in modern society.

It's obvious to me that the gender roles in today's society have drastically changed. They have changed to the point where both men and women are strapped to the working world in order to make ends meet, unfortunately advancing social and material status to a point where much of the family matrix has crumbled away.

Throughout history, men would protect and support the family, while women, including Native American women, tended to the home to benefit the family, especially children, which has been the most effective and natural way throughout the world, among all peoples, for thousands of years. By natural design, women were created and evolved as the *nurturers* for that reason.

Due to the drastic changes in today's family cultures, many kids are consequently falling through the cracks. Additionally, our elderly people are conveniently and selfishly put into nursing homes instead of being there in the family to supply daily wisdom to the other family members. What a shame, as well as a complete waste of valuable knowledge and wisdom.

As that eighth-grade make-up class went, those kids, in the end, *did* manage graduating from middle school into high school. However, that was only accomplished after picking up numerous gumball wrappers off the floor, wiping goop off everything that I had turned my back on, and fishing the virtual equivalent of tin cans, boots, and old tires out of the classroom fish tank. I tend to think previous generations, influenced by solid families, were taught better values and respect for others' property, as well as personal manners and self-discipline.

That assignment taught me, and hopefully those kids too, something about our current societal culture compared to historical cultures. As I have indicated, in our modern society, we are experiencing a serious breakdown of family structure, producing many misguided latchkey kids, with a number of these kids developing severe problems. We've also seen that without this family structure and culture in place, our future generations are in grave trouble, quickly losing the close family ties and guidance required for producing good values and principles.

Many misguided and troubled youths are sorely lacking structure, ethics, and the ability to take responsibility for their actions. Looking objectively at the whole situation, it can be seen as a family/career pendulum. Family used to take precedence over money and careers. I'm afraid just the opposite has since occurred, with the love and/or need for material gain taking parents out of the home, oftentimes permanently in the form of divorce, while leaving single-parent or no-parent households with only part-time guardians at best.

Traditionally, it's usually been the women (single mothers) who have gained custody of the children in these situations, resulting in far too many kids being raised without fathers. Additionally, many grandparents, if available and capable, are having to be involved in the full-time care of their grandkids. According to census figures, several million children in America are being raised by grandparents. I would debate that grandparents should be there to *support* and *guide* the parents, not *be* the parents.

Unless you grew up without a father (a life coach), you can't imagine the negative impact it has on one's confidence, self-esteem, and the ability to function within a highly competitive society. Unfortunately, many kids grow up struggling with these disorders their entire lives. The American Academy of Child and Adolescent Psychiatry estimates that developmental, behavioral, and mental disorders affect an estimated seven to twelve million children and adolescents at any given time in America alone.

In this highly competitive world, wrong or right, it helps to have a coach figure teaching you *how* to compete (survive) while growing up. This becomes an instinctive *survival of the fittest* requirement. However, with many people, *instinct* predominately drives them more than *intellect*, and in these cultures, this will often cause the *nice guys* to finish last. Ruthless competition and the bitter experience of consistently coming in last, escalated by a lack of instilled character, has a tendency to turn some of these *nice guys* into *not-so-nice guys* at times. In the final analysis, though, we all need to remember what we keep forgetting: *It's not whether you win or lose, but how you play the game that counts.*

Organizations like Big Brothers and Big Sisters of America are credible programs for coaching and mentoring young people, but there *is* no substitute for a father of character and integrity being around full-time while kids are growing up. Hopefully, someday, all dads will realize the critical importance of their roles within the family and will stick around for the long haul, where they're responsibly mentoring more knowledge and ethics to their children rather than primitive and competitive survival skills.

Considering women are now comprising nearly half of the workforce while being forced to compete with men for jobs, this situation only benefited big business. As it all unfolded, corporations, for the sake of profits, began to suppress the average wage to where both spouses *had* to work to make ends meet. That, in effect, may have increased the available workforce and raised the profitability and productivity levels of corporations, but it also contributed to the ongoing demise of families. Consequently, our society is now at a huge loss. Our senior citizens, often ignored, have been forced to sadly watch it all unfold on the evening news while at the same time knowing that there used to be a better way of life.

We the people need to reclaim, from big business and Washington, the primary control of our lives. We should still have faith that people banding together as informed voters and consumers are a powerful force in a democratic society, and have the full ability to control a nation and world's future. With enough knowledge and ethics, we can quit chasing our tails while complaining about and stabbing at the symptoms. Instead, we can take informed action to address the deeper root problems in order to change things for the better. The last time I looked, we people, by design, still elect the lawmakers that are representing us. Don't you think it's about time we held them fully accountable to *us* instead of big money influences?

As far as life priorities are concerned, when will people wake up and realize that *family* must take priority over possessions? Sadly, too many are guilty of getting their wires crossed when it comes to this essential value and universal principle.

The very same situation threatens our entire society. Thus, it is imperative that we teach our children proper values and principles aimed at social ethics. You can't completely get that kind of education in the public-school systems. This knowledge has to be instilled from the very beginning through early family life teachings and by well-set, living examples, especially from the elderly. Note that whenever I have referred to the word *knowledge* throughout this book, I have not merely been referring to one's abilities in academic disciplines such as math and science. Society will never be able to solve all of its problems with calculators and computers. It takes *wise choices.*

With the process of aging, there is yet

another universal principle of managing life for all of us to consider. A lot of the problems that we experience in life are often related to our level of personal freedom. Even though democracy *represents* freedom, it's usually not until people reach personal independence later in life, if then, that they finally achieve a level of *true* freedom, away from the controlling power of others.

Thoreau sarcastically wrote about the *"spending of the best part of one's life earning money in order to enjoy a questionable liberty."*

Freedom is not just rooted in the physical and mental states of our being but is relatively codetermined by our adequate financial positioning as well. Understand I'm not talking about being overly wealthy here. I'm simply talking about being financially independent to the point where creditors don't own and control us.

Up until our senior years, most of us are only technically free, and our lives are actually imprisoned by mortgages, car payments, medical bills, and other debt, supported by jobs that without which, we'd drown financially. After we finally have the ability to set ourselves free of these money monsters, we can then enjoy life for what it's meant to be, provided we still have our physical and mental health. Time itself actually plays a most crucial and important factor in this financial independence equation, since most people, not being born into money, find that it takes time and good financial planning to pull it all together in a race against the clock. Paradoxically, some people have a hard time managing their own lives, let alone their finances. Good financial planning is not only an art, as well as a science, but is also a strict habit requiring self-discipline that has to be learned and continually practiced, just like anything else worthwhile. Many will grasp and understand the concepts of good financial planning but will fail time and time again at the implementation and execution of those concepts on a personal level, due simply to a lack of knowledge and self-discipline. With time working against them, some people just can't seem to develop the willpower to implement what they may very well know but choose to ignore. For those who missed out on self-discipline training in early family life, sometimes it's not until years of experience and *self-taught* discipline that people finally manage to get their act together. Hopefully, the hourglass hasn't run out by then, and there are enough grains of sand remaining to realize their basic goals.

Financial freedom has an imperative relevance to physical freedom, in that with the aging process, people can begin to lose their physical freedom, due to their increased level of medical problems. Physically, with age, we become more and more limited as to what we can do in a coordinated manner. If we don't do things safely, we stand a good chance of not only losing our *physical* freedom but also our *financial* freedom, as observed by today's cost of health care and insurance. If one falls short on health maintenance, the cost of health care can quickly take away one's true freedom.

In the case of the aging, overall freedom is like energy; it is neither lost nor gained but merely changed from one state to another. Meaning, its possession changes from the elderly to the people who provide the goods and services that senior citizens not only want but also require. If these providers are healthcare professionals and executives, *they* may discover *their own* financial freedom on a golf course or tropical island, while the elderly lie in hospital beds, wondering how they're going to pay all the medical bills. As a senior citizen, you may just happen to find yourself lying in that hospital bed after being involved in an accident that you yourself may have contributed to, perhaps due to the onset of vision deterioration or the decreased ability to make quick decisions. Your healthcare providers' afternoon golf game might now have become a threesome or even a foursome. A lawyer or two and, perhaps, an insurance agent, may have just joined the game, and your own personal freedom could have just hooked and sliced its way down a country-club fairway.

Hopefully, you remain healthy and alert enough not to sponsor these tournaments. For senior citizens, these adverse events can be financially devastating, if not deadly.

As we get up in years, we become far more fragile and much less agile. Falling off bikes, back when we had lower profiles and were highly flexible kids, was a different world. Sure, it was still scary and it hurt, but back then, we'd usually just get back up, brush ourselves off, maybe pick a little gravel out of our knees and palms, and get right back on that unsteady mount, riding home to get some first aid, and maybe a little sympathy. As life goes on, it seems the older and bigger we get, the harder we fall, and we may not get much in the way of sympathy anymore. I can relate after crashing while biking along the Colorado River through Glenwood Canyon near a nameless town called *No Name*. That accident landed my broken bones in two different hospitals, having to undergo surgery followed by physical therapy. Even with insurance, I still had several thousand dollars of out-of-pocket medical expenses to pay. Thankfully, I had insurance that covered most of it. A lot of people don't.

As a safety-sensitive senior now, I think back to all of the situations where I could have also been seriously injured or even killed. Like the time on a mountainside when my glove got caught on the trip lever of a helicopter concrete bucket as it was soaring up and away. Luckily, the seam of my glove ripped out and dropping me before I got too far off the ground. Then there was the night I stepped on a plastic pot scrubber that my cat had left at the top of the stairs. Thankfully, all I broke while tumbling down the stairs was my tailbone and not my neck. Life doesn't always go the way we want it to. We need to anticipate and be aware of the pitfalls and hazards. In the interest of risk management, as well as aging bones, as long as there are pets around, the pot scrubber needs to go in the drawer when it's not being used.

A good lesson, hopefully learn by our senior years, and another universal principle of managing life, is that true freedom and happiness is not just reaching retirement and having a lot of money. There are things much more important than that, like your health, friends, and family. As the Beatles once sang, *"Money can't buy you love."* Although money can buy you a lot of other things, I think people are getting a little fed up with all the commercialism, especially at Christmas time. Whatever happened to the old-fashioned family Christmas? Perhaps it's time people get back to recognizing Christmas for its true spiritual and family values, rather than just going shopping for presents.

In the process of aging, I learned that one's lifestyle and personal integrity are far more important than status or material success. Moreover, we all need to keep remembering that the best things in life really are, in fact, *free;* you just need to be extra careful while doing them.

As people leave the working world, their lifestyles and living situations change. The present trend for retirees is to spend the winters in the warm south and the summers in the cool northern mountains. In either case, these retirees are mostly recreating and doing whatever retired people do to enjoy themselves *wherever* they are. Most of them carry cellular phones, have smart TVs, take in the sights and foods while traveling, and frequently sit around playing cards while discussing world events and medical ailments.

Just when we think we've planned reasonably well and have retirement all figured out, to include Social Security, that system, while being borrowed and abused by Capitol Hill, is in trouble. And with the number of people reaching retirement, one can assume that the age at which one can collect full benefits will rise and/or benefits will stagnate.

Let's think about that for a minute. What that means is, unless we have properly planned and invested for retirement, or fortunately struck it rich, we'll all now be forced to work and continue paying into Social Security or pension funds, right up until we're unable to do so or choose not to continue. Chances are, we'll have to keep working as long as we can, provided there are jobs, since the cost of living at retirement most definitely won't be getting cheaper in the future due to inflation. We can bet that members of Congress, who are exempt from the Social Security system, and having much better pension benefits, won't have to worry about *their* retirements, or their medical bills. How is it that politicians, who are supposed to be public servants, always end up on top, in comparison to the people they're supposed to serve?

The moral is, if they haven't already, people should individually start saving and investing for retirement, provided they can afford to. Either that or resign themselves to the fact that they'll be working for the rest of their capable lives or living meagerly on welfare. There may not be many other options outside of falling back on family, if available.

No doubt, with people living longer, and the laws changing, along with the level of greed and corruption in the world, unless things change, the ability of the average person to comfortably retire at a reasonable age will continue to get tougher. Sadly, for many, the *Golden Years* may not be quite so golden.

Life Exodus

The Other Side of Life
— **The Moody Blues**

We enter this world penniless, without a single possession. Inevitably, we leave it the same way. With *wise choices*, it's the footprints and impacts we leave behind that become significant.

As we finally round the corner in the final lap of this great human race, we might look back and ask ourselves, *Now, what was that all about?* Perhaps we can come up with some meaningful answers to that question.

As for myself, nearing the end of this race, even though I'm feeling a little fatigued, I believe I'm beginning to experience my second wind. That is, I think I may have finally realized many of the key principles of life.

Here's one: *It's okay to come in second, or even last, as long as your best efforts are given.*

The esoteric wisdom of the ancient Toltec, as written about by Don Miguel Ruiz, discloses four key agreements one must make in order to positively transform his or her life. The first agreement: *Be impeccable with your word.* The second: *Don't take anything personally.* Third: *Don't make assumptions.* And the fourth agreement, as I also indicated above: *Always do your best*. These principle-centered foundations of life have been tapping all people on their shoulders for centuries but have been commonly ignored by many civilizations.

Early on, while racing through life, often ignoring universal principles and truth, I spent a lot of time making mistakes, going against my own good judgment while trying to learn from those mishaps. I'm confident, provided I make *wise choices* from here on out, that I will take notice of those truths and no longer make the same mistakes.

Additionally, throughout the race, I believe that I have learned to deal with adversity, knowing that things can always be worse.

Most of all, I hope that by the time I head down that final straightaway in a sprint toward the finish line, I have become a person that values and respects others as well as myself. At that, it's best to finish the race *in service* of others rather than in a self-serving manner. After all, we can't exactly finish the last leg of this race until we have officially passed the baton to those who can most benefit from our experiences as well as our many years of instilled knowledge. I strongly feel that all of us are put in this world as a test. What we do with that level of responsibility becomes a personal choice, for which we will somehow be graded in the end. Like a final exam, many will pass, some will fail, and few will excel.

I have learned that, in many cases, service

occupations that may not pay well oftentimes are the most rewarding. Occupation does not necessarily signify profession. In the case of teaching, it may be professional but marginally lucrative. Volunteer work is non-lucrative but can be highly rewarding.

One of the most rewarding experiences of my life was the eight days I spent as a volunteer, working double shifts with the American Red Cross during a large forest fire that forced the evacuation of over 1,700 homes. As fate would have it, on the second day of providing community service, I became an evacuee myself. At no time are people brought closer than during a disaster. On the final day of my service, I had numerous people thank me for my help. I also had an elderly lady ask me if I attended church. My reply to her was; *Rarely*, but that I had just spent the last eight days there.

In retrospect, as I stood by and watched my neighbors scramble to load their most valuable possessions into their vehicles by flashlight that thick, smokey night when the power went off, I came to further understand a basic value in life; I gained a greater appreciation that without friends, family, and faith, we are all alone in this world. In the midst of a disaster, one comes to fully appreciate the true meaning of life. Adversity acts to reinforce our values. That fire, coincidentally named *The Missionary Ridge Fire*, taught our whole community an important lesson.

In the course of this life, I've had other meaningful lessons handed to me while learning to look up to individuals who were excellent role models to guide me along the way. One of them was Viktor Frankl who was persecuted in the holding camps during the Nazi Holocaust, simply because of his ethnic origin. He survived the depths of inhumanity. His example points to that spark in the human spirit that chooses to survive. Against all odds, he did survive, and his life stands as a powerful symbol to all who face adversity. Viktor Frankl lived to write one of the most inspirational books ever written – *Man's Search for Meaning*. It was Frankl who said, "*Everything can be taken from a man but…the last of the human freedoms – to choose one's attitude in any given set of circumstances.*"

Prejudice, as an example of bad attitude, has a very nasty way of destroying innocent lives. From a management perspective, prejudice can be looked upon as a cause-and-effect relationship. The effects of prejudice create the rejection, degradation, and persecution of others. Hate, anger, and jealousy are the symptoms which bring us to the root cause of prejudice, being the lack of true knowledge and understanding gained from childhood conditioning and education. Parents and teachers have a great deal of responsibility to lead children in ethical and principled directions.

Deloris Jordan, the mother of basketball superstar Michael Jordan, claimed that her son's most amazing accomplishments were actually made outside of the basketball court. She indicated that she was most proud that her son was a caring, decent human being who strived to treat everyone he met with respect. In Deloris's own words, she said, *"I don't care how much money you have; you can't buy character. If it hasn't been instilled in you, you haven't got it."*

Although we must take risks in life to get anywhere, all risks are choices and have calculated odds of success. Some choices are smart, some are foolish. It's obviously to our advantage to make *wise choices*. In the end, people who have chosen to not take calculated risks for fear of failure, who have consequently led sheltered lives, may have missed out on life itself. For those who took a chance, hopefully, the risks paid out, resulting in a positive outcome, and were not aimed at taking advantage of or hurting others.

I've learned, through my own search for meaning, that knowledge is not only a form of power, but that, through knowledge, we obtain freedom of choice as well as freedom from our own fears. With that level of freedom, we can finally obtain peace of mind. So, with enough knowledge, all of us working together realistically have the ability to establish everlasting peace on this planet. If it can be envisioned, it can be accomplished.

If humanity is going to survive, people,

young and old, rich and poor, no matter their religion, have to become better educated and more responsible. It is, therefore, relevant to restate an important point made in this book: We, as individual members of a democratic society, need to use our hearts and our heads, ethics, instead of our special interests while making decisions. In doing so, we should not believe every paid political ad that we hear or see in the media. Instead, we should use our own ability to think critically, along with thorough research and understanding of the issues, before we make up our minds and prematurely or prejudicially decide upon anything.

Unfortunately, we, the human race, continue to remain in somewhat of a quandary or paradox when it comes to the required level of knowledge to make *wise choices*. Albert Einstein said it best when he declared, "*Only two things are infinite – the universe and human stupidity, and I'm not so sure about the universe.*"

Historically, as well as recently, people of the world, in general, have pretentiously masqueraded themselves as being intelligent, when in actuality we're far from it. If people were intelligent, we would stop fighting each other. Instead, we would put our heads and hearts together and solve the world's problems. When and if we ever get to that point, we can then earn the right to call ourselves intelligent.

I've learned that human relationships, in or

out of families, are extremely fragile. Like Humpty Dumpty, if broken, they can hardly be fully put back together again. Relationships can also be looked at like pieces of machinery, which have to be well designed from the beginning and built according to specific plans. Once in operation, they need to be continually maintained through a well-managed process to avoid breakdowns. Moreover, in the event of a breakdown, they must be properly repaired. In comparison, without proper design, maintenance, and repair, relationships will suffer probable replacement when their life expectancy and perceived usefulness have ended. Divorce is a prime example of relationships that have become rusted and ceased, unable to function due to a lack of proper design and/or care.

Considering that we are all imperfect human beings, as with critical machines, we require quality regulatory agencies in our lives, be it ethical government, including spirituality, as quality control measures to keep us on the right track. I'm just not sure if we, as a society, can put our differences and special interests aside long enough to reach a point where we can actually govern ourselves in a completely impartial and ethical manner. Selfish ideologies are acting to destroy everything of true value that democracy has worked and fought so hard to create.

America and the rest of the Free World are in trouble. Our future quality of life hangs in the balance. If we're ever going to do it, the time has come to turn this ship around. Unless we want to deal with frequent disasters in our lives, we had all better sit up and take notice of what's going on around us, getting involved and committed to preserving the environment and improving life for everyone.

So, do get involved. Start voicing well informed, intelligent opinions. Get out and vote. Volunteer in service of others. Become an activist for ethics in both business and government. Don't just sit there like a frog in hot water while the temperature rises around us. Do something – before it's too late. We need to head off disasters.

One of my favorite quotes related to disasters and quality of life is from the renowned quality control expert, Juran, who proclaimed, *"The phenomenon of life behind the quality dikes requires that we provide good quality to shield society against service interruptions and to guard against disasters."*

That particular quote works for machines as well as governments, organizations, and personal relationships. In that respect, it's all of our responsibility to start qualitatively plugging that leaky dike. No matter how much quality control we put into something, with people not being perfect, there will always be room for improvement. In many cases, we don't seem to be headed in the qualitative direction that we should be.

Outside of the principle of instilling ethics in young people, brings me to another important principle of managing life: *Balanced physical, mental, and spiritual wellness*. No individual will ever achieve true happiness through material possessions. People may claim and perceive themselves to be physically and mentally happy, but spiritually, they may be missing that altogether. In the end, no one person can ever spiritually arrive at the summit of Mt. Happiness, all by himself or herself, as long as there are others who are suffering down below in the world. I'm talking about those who are without the basic necessities of life, whatever they may be – physical or emotional.

The ascent that I'm describing makes Mt. Everest pale by comparison. The members of the expedition are all of us – you, me, everyone. Furthermore, like climbing Mt. Everest, this expedition will never reach the summit without the cooperation and efforts of the entire team. No one can be excluded, and there are no excuses for not capably participating. It is by far the most important challenge that society has ever had to make. And unethical competition, while exploiting each other, is completely against the rules.

There was a time when early generations sealed contracts in *trust* with just a handshake. Today, you might be considered a *fool* for doing that, with no way to implement a lawsuit in case of damages.

How do you think we became a culture where no one picks up hitchhikers anymore? In big cities, most people can't even look strangers in the eye in public, for fear of being preyed upon.

I'm reminded of the time I came across a baby bird that had obviously fallen from its nest, becoming suddenly vulnerable to a world of predators. Not being able to locate the nest, there was little I could do. If I dared touch the baby bird, the mother might abandon it, if she hadn't already. I realized that this was a common situation in the wild and chose to leave the expertise of Nature to deal with it – good or bad. I knew the mother, if still available, would fearlessly give up her own life in the effort to protect her offspring. Natural instincts and survival of the fittest would dictate the outcome. Wild animals don't have a choice in these situations; however, people do.

Think about all the suffering that unhealthy, poor people have endured while being preyed upon by segments of our society like the medical, pharmaceutical, and insurance industry. Not to mention the other rapidly rising costs of living on top of that. I was reading *Time Magazine*, when I came across what I perceived to be a professional article on mental health, written by the Surgeon General of the United States. Only after reading and studying the entire article, including the fine print, did I realize it to be a paid advertisement by the pharmaceutical industry. They call it health care. I wonder how much *care* this article actually reflected. Or was it just a deception to sell a product to the unsuspecting?

According to the health insurance industry, pharmaceutical advertising, heavily targeted at ordinary people, has tripled in the United States in recent years. Accordingly, drug usage has grown at the same rate, and due to the laws of supply and demand, so have the profit margins of the pharmaceutical companies. Coincidentally, I came across that distressed baby bird the very same day I read that false article. I believe Nature to be a valuable mentor to all of us, provided we have the *wisdom* to sit up and take notice. The problem is, too many people in the Free World haven't recently cared about anyone but themselves and their bank accounts. Lack of care has led to lack of trust. We've all heard the phrase; *Nobody cares how much you know until they know how much you care*. Caring leads to trust. We can no longer trust each other, individually or as a society, any more than we can trust hitchhikers and solicitors.

The world needs to educate itself and change its mindset. People need to be mentally reconditioned to not only trust *in* others, but more importantly, to also be trustworthy *of* others. Society has to start to genuinely *care* about each other to the point where *untrustworthy* people become an inconsequential minority, not tolerated by the ethical majority.

Currently, with misleading advertisements, the psychiatric and pharmaceutical world has not been able to always fix or maintain our lives for us, no matter how much they keep telling us they can. Do you think Viktor Frankl got through the Holocaust with the help of a psychiatrist and antidepressants? No, he got through it with sheer determination, self-discipline, and freedom of choice. Instilled character and integrity, along with faith and self-discipline, becomes a person's psychological immune system.

Using nature as an example, like baby birds, we can tragically leave the nest by accident. Unlike other animals, however, we humans can return to the nest through our own determination and faith. Out of the nest, we can be eaten alive in this world, but with enough faith and the ability to make *wise choices* in life, we can protect ourselves from untrustworthy predators who don't care about anyone but themselves.

America's twenty-eighth president, Woodrow Wilson, once said, *"Love lives not in oneself but in the object of that love."* On an emotional level, some will emphatically claim that they give, as well as receive, unconditional love and respect from others, only to find themselves in the process of abandoning and neglecting once-loved ones and/or friends or being abandoned and neglected themselves. Rejection and abandonment are powerful emotions.

Unconditional love, including that love supposedly found in families, sometimes has a strange way of transforming itself into negative and selfish actions. The end result is rejection, where people become unaccepted by others for who and what they are for prejudicial reasons. As I've indicated, the recent divorce and relationship/friendship dumping rate, as well as the number of private clubs and so-called cliques in the world would support this kind of reasoning. Love builds us up. Hate breaks us down.

As for unconditional love and respect, outside of a parent's love for their own children, there is more of it between people and their pets than there is between one human being and another in the world. Infants and pets, for example, are totally accepting and dependent upon their parent/owners for everything they need or want. Therefore, there is no challenge for power and control in the relationship. The parent/owners possess all of the uncontested power. Consequently, unconditional love and respect from the top down, as well as from the bottom up, is natural in these particular situations. Your dog would never challenge the power and authority you have over him, would he? On the other hand, as in parenting and teaching, older children oftentimes will, provided you let them.

Where there is a lack or breakdown of unconditional love and respect, there are always undeniable power struggles going on, be it between countries, families, friends, associates, or spouses. Witness the breakdown of unconditional love and respect between some parents and their teenage children; outside of many dysfunctional situations, such as alcoholism, domestic violence, abuse, etc., power struggles can be a major cause of it. When teens start to flex their own freedom, parents or guardians will usually begin to resist, since allowing it involves having to give up some of their own personal power, or because they know that without guidance, teens are much more at risk. Children will only obtain the power they crave when adults either give it to them, or when they finally become nondependent and self-sufficient. This often happens prematurely with teenagers who no longer want to tolerate the rules at home, laid down by their parents, so they voluntarily or involuntarily leave home. However, some parents, even in these situations, will continue to hold certain forms of power over their children, be it material or psychological.

Accordingly, power struggles, while they're happening, are nothing more than political tugs-of-war. Certain parents and teens will relate well to what I'm saying. The trouble with many of our young people today is that they have been given, as well as taken, too much power (freedom), when they're not actually responsible enough to handle it. I sometimes wonder if grownups have obtained too much freedom as well, in proportion to personal levels of responsibility and maturity.

As with all forms of disagreement, people do have a choice as to the outcome in these relationship battles. Attempting to understand and to care about the other's point of view is always a *wise choice.* However, people, being less than perfect, don't always make good choices in life and are often less than capable of effectively managing themselves or their families without governing guidance and intervention. As an example, adults who are devoid of character are at a loss when trying to instill character in their children. As Michael Jordan's mother stated, *"Money cannot buy what we're talking about."* Money won't follow us out of this life, but our spiritual souls will.

In the first chapter, I supported the likely existence of a superior Being or Force that manages the universe. Many religions throughout history have referred to this figure as God. Some circles refer to it as the Master(s) of the Universe. To the Buddhists, there is not only God, but also the Christlike equivalency of *Buddha.* For people devoted to Islam, there is the supreme Allah. The Native Americans have always displayed a deep spiritual respect for Mother Earth or Nature itself. Even nonreligious people may indirectly find themselves, at times, referring to a natural force called *karma,* which means; *As you sow, so shall you reap.* Or, another way to put it; *What goes around, comes around.* You may not believe in a superior Being or Force, but at the same time, you may alternatively find yourself believing in *Lady Luck*. Religions of different civilizations, even with all their differences, still have distinct threads of commonality. The Bhagavad Gita and the Upanishads, ancient spiritual writings dating back to the second century BC, represent for the Hindu basically what the Old and New Testaments of the Bible represent for Christians. Still, in these ancient writings, there are common values and universal principles, found in each of them, that have guided civilizations for thousands of years and have survived both the scrutiny and the test of time. Like the laws of physics, if these unwavering principles and steadfast values were not, in fact, valid and true, they would have been discarded by humanity ages ago. Ultimately, in the final scheme of things, there must be truth in the common aspects of these beliefs. Thoreau spiritually wrote the following:

"Nearest to all things is that power which fashions their being. Next to us the grandest laws are continually being executed. Next to us is not the workman whom we have hired, with whom we love so well to talk, but the workman whose work we are."

People may claim, *I'm spiritual, I'm just not religious.* That said, we might believe there is someone or something of power overseeing everything, but we simply choose not to be a part of any formalized religion. The magazine *Spirituality & Health* once did a poll, asking people in America about religion and spirituality. Over half of the respondents, 59 percent, described themselves as both religious *and* spiritual. Twenty percent, or one in five, saw themselves as only spiritual. I'm assuming the remaining 21 percent were neither religious *nor* spiritual. The majority of people taking the survey, who admitted their faith, saw God as being everywhere and in everything, rather than someone somewhere above us. Interestingly, 80 percent of those respondents believed that parenting is a spiritual activity. Additionally, 67 percent considered a walk in the forest to be a divine experience. So, taking your kids for a walk in the forest stands to be a worthwhile pursuit.

Whatever the religious or nonreligious belief, there is undoubtedly a unique common denominator to this equation – a golden thread that connects everyone and everything together. So why on earth do we knowingly choose to continue fighting among ourselves either physically or psychologically? It doesn't make intelligent sense.

Faced with devastating illnesses, traumatic experiences, or a sudden brush with death itself, many people, religious or not, will find themselves preoccupied in some sort of reverent meditation or prayer. The time just prior to the possibility or probability of death, facing one's mortality is most likely the strongest spiritual event or experience of anyone's life. During World War II, a popular phrase was; *There are no atheists in foxholes*. I would safely assume that many of the thousands of people who suddenly faced their inevitable death in New York City on September 11, 2001, might have had spiritual thoughts of desperation or fear in those final moments.

Death itself may very well be the threshold of our awareness as to what actually exists beyond the physical world. For truly peaceful people, I suspect the moment of death may be a form of blissful nirvana. Conversely, for unethical and ruthless people, perhaps a rude awakening. Could there really be a heaven or hell? Perhaps, but they may not be what we think they are. Although, there must be something to this dichotomy of *good* and *evil*.

Thinking about it, the world and universe are obviously two sided – big/small, up/down, hot/cold, yes and no. There are dynamic duos wherever you look, no matter which way you turn – light/dark, right/left, open/closed, in/out, positive and negative. And of course, as with life, the beginning and the end, birth and death (*Life Genesis* and *Life Exodus*). Likewise, the very heart of computer language is based on two opposing binary codes – zero and one. An interesting concept to ponder. Someday, people may better understand the true meaning of this universal principle. According to Mahatma Gandhi, *"All contrary qualities are attributed to God because we cannot free our minds from dualities."*

As a theory, there may actually be two opposing universes operating in different dimensions. What if the one we're presently living in happens to be the *negative* dimension of the two, where there are wars, natural disasters, disease, famine, depression, a lack of goodwill, deprivation, suffering, and pain? Maybe there's a parallel world or *heaven* somewhere out there in another dimension. In which case, *hell* might just be a place all too familiar to us. Shakespear once said; *"Hell is empty and all the devils are here."* Perhaps we can never leave the incarnations of *this* world until we actually become worthy of the other, like negative electrons confined within a battery, eventually released by a power switch, allowed to flow toward a positive force. Death following a principled life may be that switch.

Albert Einstein, in the course of his life, discovered one of the secrets of the universe in relation to energy. He discovered that energy equates to mass multiplied by the speed of light squared or ($E=MC^2$). This means that all matter has to be associated with a *huge* amount of energy. According to the equation, there's a direct relationship between matter, its energy, and the speed of light. Only recently have scientists been able to actually control the speed of light. In fact, in these controlled situations, they have been able to almost stop or even accelerate light to a speed beyond its traditional speed.

Not being a physicist, I'm not sure how it all works. However, I think there are a few missing pieces of the puzzle or equation that Einstein never completed, yet to be discovered as science advances. I think one of those missing puzzle pieces has something to do with *time* itself and the *spiritual* dimension. In that respect, *everlasting life* may actually be possible in the spiritual realm.

When and if we discover these remaining, hidden secrets of the universe, will people accept it? Perhaps the human race has that knowledge buried somewhere deep in our combined subconscious minds. Carl Jung called it *the collective unconscious.*

Throughout history, most of it recent, we have continually unlocked one secret after another and have a much better understanding of things, *collectively.* Each of us alone is relatively ignorant in this process, but together, we're making progress. Though we've barely scratched the surface of these discoveries and have only begun putting the puzzle together, my fear is that we will never have either the time or the patience to fully finish it, since we're much too preoccupied. Maybe that's where AI comes in. Nevertheless, I'll wager that the puzzle I'm referring to will be a pretty amazing sight to behold when all of the pieces come together.

Just as our pets cannot begin to imagine technology as we know it, it stands to reason that many things we humans cannot yet sense or understand more than likely exist. Though our pets are not rocket scientists any more than most people are, we humans at least have enough intelligence to know that rocket science exists; our pets don't. In fact, our pets are incapable of even wonder about it. That is what separates humans from the rest of the animal kingdom and from each other – different levels of intelligence. So, yes, there are undoubtedly things about the universe that we as humans don't remotely even suspect. We may presently be incapable of supreme wisdom and truth, but perhaps we may eventually advance and evolve to a point where we can begin to have further awareness of it. There *is* hope. Astronomers, with tools like the Hubbell telescope, and the James Webb Space Telescope, have been able to sneak a peek at some truly amazing things out there. Stay tuned, we haven't seen *anything* yet.

Back in Chapter Three, dealing with formative youth, I mentioned the heightened sense of awareness that kids at that age experience. Nowhere throughout the rest of our lives is the sense of exploring so vivid, or the ability to see, smell, hear, feel, and taste so distinct. Our experiences and partnerships with Nature start to sever themselves, due to our man-made environments, after we pass those formative years. What used to be second nature to us as kids, paying full attention to Nature while using all of our senses, becomes secondary in our now busy, adult lives.

In these natural settings, there is a unique experience to life, as long as we're out actually experiencing it from time to time and not cooped up inside continually surfing the Internet, watching television, or anchored to some other unnatural setting. Most modern people today are living sheltered lives with diminished senses, not being able to recall the insight of having a full-alert spectrum of this natural awareness and how wonderful being in tune with Nature can be.

In the mid-1800s, Thoreau, being fairly spiritual, spent two years in isolated union with nature, while living at Walden Pond in Concord, Massachusetts. As a result, he created some of the most remarkable thoughts in literary history. To this day, Thoreau's introspections, associated with his alliance with Nature and conservation, continue to have a profound influence on our world.

Anyone who truly understands Nature can walk through the wilderness completely alone, while at the same time be surrounded by natural as well as spiritual friends.

The message here is that it may be time for the world to come to its natural and spiritual senses. The universal puzzle that I've described will never be solved by a society wasting its time sitting around in hot water, playing video games, texting, or watching sitcoms and commercials on TV. In today's noisy, unnatural world of commercialism, consumerism, and materialism, the silence of the natural world can barely be heard, if at all. One cannot spiritually hear its messages being whispered to us while surrounded by and indulged in a noisy man-made environment. Meditation therefore has great value. I fully believe there is, in fact, a sixth sense. Perhaps there is even a seventh, or more. Who really knows for sure?

Unless we continue to advance our combined level of sensitive intelligence, we will only be self-perceived as intelligent people, while in reality we're actually ignorant of what's really going on around us at the universal or spiritual levels. What a shame for so many generations of people to reach the end of their lives, not really knowing, understanding, or even caring what it was that they just experienced and why. Like a housecat sitting in a window looking out, even though the cat may see things of interest, like birds and bugs, little does it realize the vast world beyond that.

Education is the gateway to knowledge, and knowledge, coupled with experience, is the gateway to wisdom. Upon leaving graduate school, I had the opportunity to sponsor and purchase one of the many brick pavers in front of the new library at Regis University in Denver. In doing this, I was allowed to have inscribed anything appropriate that I wanted upon it. As far as I know, that brick still holds its unique place within that very walkway. The inscription on it simply reads:

Education is Peace.

I used the word *education* in that particular application instead of the word *knowledge*, because of its setting at the entrance to a university. Obviously both words are highly related in meaning, but what goes on behind the doors of schools, colleges, and universities is *education*. What emerges from those doors, with time, is *knowledge*. If there had only been more room on that brick, I would have had inscribed the following:

With education and experience comes knowledge and wisdom. With knowledge and wisdom comes peace and goodwill...and with that comes exactly what all of humanity has been truly longing for throughout history.

Like the minds of so many people, in relation to the universe, it's too bad that brick was so small.

Until all people in the world can put a lid on prejudice and the hatred that results, I'm afraid that we'll continue to go through the future as just a bunch of so-called brick-heads – a descriptive and befitting term often used for unknowledgeable people who make less than *wise choices* in life.

Despite our individual battles with evil and temptation, day in and day out, can we ever learn to overcome prejudice, hate, and greed to the point where we stop killing each other, lying to each other, cheating each other, and stealing from each other? Moreover, can we learn to stop setting bad examples for children? The answer to all of the above is a resounding *Yes, we can*! We inherently, within ourselves, have the power as well as the ability to create a new and positive world. *Yes, we can* suppress and extinguish our physical acts of anger, evil instincts, and tempting influences, but it will take us making *wise choices*.

War, murder, and other forms of violence can no longer be tolerated in an intelligent society. *Yes, we can* prevent children from entering penal institutions through instilled knowledge and understanding through proper upbringings. Additionally, through awareness education, we can also expel a number of existing convicts out of our prisons to become positive, productive, and trustworthy members of society. It's been done before. What we're doing now to deter murders and violent crimes is obviously not working. All we are experiencing is increasingly overcrowded prison conditions, with almost two million predominately male prisoners being inefficiently detained at the expense of the rest of society.

Further considering the essence of life, one of the greatest minds on that subject was Abraham Maslow. Maslow originated the idea that a hierarchy of physical requirements leads to an ultimate humanistic identity called *self-actualization* – the ability to actualize psychological and spiritual needs above and beyond the basic physical needs. The hierarchy was modeled as a pyramid with the primary foundational needs being *physiological*, such as food, clothing, and shelter. Higher on the pyramid, the next level of needs is *psychological*, such as family, friends, community, rewarding occupations, self-confidence, and self-esteem.

Considering rewarding occupations, Maslow pointed out that people working for organizations would not be content or highly productive until they were allowed to reach this upper level of self-actualization. You can lead workers to tools of trade, but you can't make them excel unless they're motivated to do so.

After giving this theory much study and thought, I fully agree with Maslow. However, I would advance the theory to include a *fourth* dimensional sphere that envelops the three-dimensional pyramid. This sphere, I would propose, represents the combined subconscious and spiritual part of our minds, perhaps the energy state of our being; the soul, if you will.

Now, the hierarchy becomes complete. We then have a full model – body, mind, *and* spirit. The pyramid of body and mind, as a metaphor, is noticeable as everyday conscious life; however, the spiritual sphere around it remains consciously invisible but intuitively real.

With this complete model representation (the visible and the invisible), we can now begin to understand an important principal that American society was founded upon – freedom of religion (spiritualism). The nation's forefathers were on the right track; they just couldn't actually see or prove that one of the two rails America was riding on actually existed, so they gave its citizens the inalienable right to believe in it if they chose to. A growing and prevalent lack of faith that the other rail actually exists is precisely why the Free World is now facing moral derailment. The *moral majority*, as it used to be referred to, is rapidly headed in the direction of becoming a minority, if it hasn't already.

Maslow was correct in the visible part of his three-dimensional model. But the all-encompassing sphere in the fourth dimension was missing simply because mortals could not actually detect it with their conscious minds or any existing scientific instruments. That doesn't mean it's not real.

Conclusively, life is not fulfilled or complete without the full trilogy in place. In fact, it's quite empty and void of substance. One has to exercise and care for all three components of the physical, mental, and spiritual being to become a completely happy, healthy, loving person.

Hopefully, the day will come when all of humanity will cease being oblivious, while obtaining true wisdom, along with the ability to not only survive but thrive. Perhaps then, all people will finally develop an awareness of the invisible sphere of energy located in the other dimension around the pyramid of our physical and mental existence. When that day arrives, the world will finally stop fighting, *wisely choosing* to lay down its weapons in everlasting peace.

It, therefore, becomes a worldwide choice as well as an obligation for people to live with principled integrity, self-discipline, ethics, and a sense of responsibility to reach out a genuinely concerned hand of care and respect toward others. For centuries we've been well advised to *love one another.* The time has come to take that advice to heart.

We, the people, in the interest of physical survival, mental happiness, spiritual fulfillment, and *love*, should continue to strive vigorously in the ongoing search for truth and wisdom.

After all, knowledge is not only *power*...

Better than riches, ***Knowledge is Peace.***

www.ingramcontent.com/pod-product-compliance
Lightning Source LLC
Chambersburg PA
CBHW070105290526
45789CB00005B/1935